More praise for Dave Barry and *Dave Barry Is Not Taking This Sitting Down!*

Also by Dave Barry

THE TAMING OF THE SCREW
BABIES AND OTHER HAZARDS OF SEX
STAY FIT AND HEALTHY UNTIL YOU'RE DEAD
CLAW YOUR WAY TO THE TOP
BAD HABITS
DAVE BARRY'S GUIDE TO MARRIAGE AND/OR SEX
HOMES AND OTHER BLACK HOLES
DAVE BARRY'S GREATEST HITS
DAVE BARRY SLEPT HERE
DAVE BARRY TURNS 40
DAVE BARRY TALKS BACK
DAVE BARRY'S ONLY TRAVEL GUIDE
   YOU'LL EVER NEED
DAVE BARRY DOES JAPAN
DAVE BARRY IS *NOT* MAKING THIS UP
DAVE BARRY'S GIFT GUIDE TO END ALL GIFT GUIDES
DAVE BARRY'S COMPLETE GUIDE TO GUYS
DAVE BARRY IN CYBERSPACE
DAVE BARRY'S BOOK OF BAD SONGS
DAVE BARRY IS FROM MARS *AND* VENUS
DAVE BARRY TURNS 50
BIG TROUBLE

DAVE BARRY

IS NOT TAKING THIS

SITTING DOWN!

Illustrations by Jeff MacNelly

BALLANTINE BOOKS • NEW YORK

A Ballantine Book
Published by The Random House Publishing Group
Copyright © 2000 by Dave Barry

www.ballantinebooks.com

ISBN 0-345-44409-4

This edition published by arrangement with Crown Publishers, a division of Random House, Inc.

Manufactured in the United States of America

Cover Photographs by Bill Wax

First Ballantine Books Trade Edition: November 2001
First Ballantine Books Mass Market Edition: August 2002

OPM 10 9 8 7 6 5 4 3

CONTENTS

Introduction

People often ask me: "Dave, what is the best thing about being a professional humor columnist?"

I always answer: "The best thing is that I can help others and make the world a better place."

Then everybody has a hearty laugh, because, of course, I am lying. In fact, that's one of the great things about being a humor columnist: You can lie! You get PAID to lie! What other profession can say that?

OK, lawyers. But they have to wear suits. Whereas we humor columnists can wear whatever we want. We could report to work in a giant squirrel costume, and our employers would not question it. They might even be impressed by it, and remark upon it positively in our annual Job Performance Review. ("Shows good initiative. Came to work in squirrel costume.")

When you are a professional humor columnist, people cut you a large amount of slack. I have an office at *The Miami Herald*, a serious, major metropolitan newspaper. Here are some of the items that I keep in that office:

—A six-foot-tall plastic-foam model of a bear (named "Bob");
—A plastic bag containing the preserved reproductive system of an actual cow (named "Bossy");
—A huge mutant corn-flake wad in a display case;

—A reproduction of Leonardo da Vinci's painting *The Last Supper,* with a clock in it;

—A rubber chicken wearing underpants;

—An electronic gun that can make a burping noise, a puking noise, a farting noise, and *all three noises combined;*

—An extensive collection of beers, including Old Jock Strong Ale, Bone Beer, St. George Lager ("Traditional Ethiopian Flavor"), Louie's Evil Lager, and Blade Beer ("Official Brew of the World Famous Lawn Rangers from Amazing Arcola, Ill.");

—Two cans of "Potted Meat Food Product," each at least 10 years old;

—A picture of a man lifting 350 pounds *with his private parts;*

. . . and much, *much* more. And guess what? Nobody thinks it's odd that I have these items in my office. Because it's *not* odd. These are all *work-related items.* I obtained every one of them in the course of doing my job as a professional humor columnist. They are the Tools of My Trade!

My point is that I have a wonderful job. It's WAY better than other so-called "prestige" jobs, such as neurosurgeon or president of the United States. Don't believe me? Let's compare the key elements of the three professions:

	Neurosurgeon	President of United States	Humor Columnist
OK to wear squirrel costume to work?	No	Only on special occasions	Yes
Hardest part of job	Drilling into skull of live human	Maintaining delicate balance of peace in world	Working phrase "weasel boogers" into column

	Neurosurgeon	President of United States	Humor Columnist
Worst that can happen	Brains squirt onto your shoes	Nuclear war wipes out civilization	Phrase "weasel boogers" fails to appear in column
Ultimate benefit	Can save a life	Can truly make the world a better place for millions of people	Can drink beer on job

So the facts are clear: By any objective standard of measurement, there is no better profession than humor columnist. That is why so many people want my job. It looks so easy! In fact, as you read the columns in this book, you may find yourself thinking: "Hey, *I* could do this. *Any* random person could do this!"

That is where you are wrong, my friend. It takes a very special *kind* of random person to be a humor columnist. Every year, hundreds of thousands of people try their hand at this demanding profession. After a few months, almost all of them have given up and gone back to the ninth grade.

Do you think you could do this job? Do you have what it takes to be a truly *professional* humor columnist? To find out, take the following multiple-choice quiz:

TEST OF YOUR HUMOR-COLUMNIST APTITUDE

1. The part of the newspaper that you turn to first is:
   a. The front page.
   b. The editorial page.
   c. The page that says what time *The Simpsons* is on.

2. The primary purpose of a newspaper column is to:
   a. Inform the readers about all sides of important issues.

    b. Change readers' minds through reasoned argument.

    c. Contain the phrase "weasel boogers."

3. What is the best resource to consult when confirming a fact?

    a. The encyclopedia.

    b. The Internet.

    c. Confirming a *what*?

4. As a journalist, you should always carry a notepad because it enables you to:

    a. Accurately recall conversations and events.

    b. Maintain a record of your research.

    c. Remove food wads trapped between your teeth.

5. If you were given the opportunity to ask one question of the Pope, what would that question be?

    a. "What do you hope will be your legacy to future generations?"

    b. "What is the greatest moral threat facing humanity today?"

    c. "Can I wear your hat?"

6. You write a column containing a so-called "joke" that is so tasteless, insensitive, juvenile, vicious, and cruel that thousands of readers write or call the newspaper to state that they are deeply offended. You should:

    a. Apologize to them in a column.

    b. Apologize to them in a public forum.

    c. Threaten to cancel their subscriptions.

SCORING: If you answered "c" to all of these questions, then you might have potential as a humor columnist. But I warn you: There is a lot of work involved.

For example, in this book you'll find two columns I wrote about Paris. To produce those two columns, I had to spend *two weeks* in Paris conducting tax-deductible research in various cafés so I could provide my readers with solid information about issues such as exactly where Paris is (not in Italy, it turns out) and what the French people are thinking (they're thinking that we're morons).

You will find that quality of research oozing out of every column in this book. I hope you enjoy it and learn from it. Because my goal, in writing it, was to help others and make the world a better place.

A Few Words About the Title

A tremendous amount of thought went into choosing a title for this book. My personal choice, designed to appeal to the book-buying impulses of today's consumer, was: Tuesdays with Harry Potter.

Unfortunately, the Legal Department had some problems with that. So eventually we decided to go with *Dave Barry Is Not Taking This Sitting Down!* This title was selected for two reasons:

1. It reflects the fact that, while on a superficial level, this work may appear to be "humorous," its underlying theme, its *raison d'être,* is the expression of deep concern—and, yes, outrage—about the forces of ignorance, injustice, oppression, and profound moral decay that beset American society today.
2. It meant we could put a toilet on the cover.

So there I was, sitting under the hot lights, when suddenly Vicki Lawrence leaped to her feet and started yelling at me about the death penalty. This happened in Los Angeles, on the TV show *Politically Incorrect*. People yell a lot on that show. One time I was on there with Micky Dolenz; he yelled at me, too. Back when I used to watch The Monkees on TV, I never dreamed that one day, one of them would be yelling at me personally regarding current events. This is a great nation.

Guests are encouraged to express strong views on *Politically Incorrect*, because it makes for better entertainment. The host, Bill Maher, could name any topic at all—say, monetary reform in the 17th-century Netherlands—and we guests would immediately be at each other's throats over it, even if we were not totally certain what "Netherlands" are.

I was on *Politically Incorrect* because I was on a book tour. You go on whatever show they tell you to go on, in hopes that the host will at some point hold your book up to the camera, causing consumers all over America to rush to bookstores to purchase it. You will basically do anything to get your book on TV. For example, a few days earlier, I let a total stranger commit a major act of gel on my hair. This was on *The Today Show*, in New York. I was sitting in the makeup room, drinking coffee, trying to wake up, and the makeup person, after studying my head, called the hair person over, pointed at my hair, and said: "See? This is exactly what I was talking about."

Then they both laughed, and the hair person, before I knew what was happening, applied 37 pounds of Industrial Concrete Strength gel in my hair, and thus I appeared on national television looking like Eddie Munster. This would have been fine if the reaction of the world at large had been to rush out and purchase my book, but the actual reaction, to judge from the people I know who saw the show, was to ask: "What happened to your hair?"

But getting back to Vicki Lawrence: She was yelling at me about the death penalty, and I was yelling back at her, while simultaneously—and I am NOT proud of this—holding my hand over the mouth of another guest, Sol Wachtler, a former chief judge of the New York State Court of Appeals who got into trouble over a woman and went to jail and, needless to say, wrote a book. I was silencing him so that I could better express my very strongly held views on the death penalty, although now I honestly cannot remember what those specific views were.

I do remember that before the show, when I was in the waiting room with Vicki Lawrence, somebody brought up her hit song, "The Night the Lights Went Out in Georgia," which has an extremely complicated plot. I have never met anybody who understood what that song is about, so I figured this was my big chance to find out.

"What is that song about?" I asked Vicki Lawrence.

"I have absolutely no idea," she said.

Here's a coincidence: Vicki Lawrence was once a regular on *The Carol Burnett Show*, and earlier that same day, I met: Carol Burnett! Yes! A comedy goddess! A star who, in my mind, is bigger than all the ex-Monkees *combined*. She and I were waiting to appear on the early-morning news show on Los Angeles TV station KTLA. I still don't know why Carol Burnett was there; I don't think she has a book out. I do know that we were both preceded on the show by a lengthy live news report in which the reporter wound up stripping down to her bathing suit and—I am not making this up—taking a shower with a live iguana. I don't know whether the iguana has a book out, but I would not bet against it.

The next day I was on a show called *Home & Family*, which is broadcast from a house on the Universal Studios lot, just a short distance from the house where Tony Perkins stabbed Janet Leigh to death in *Psycho*. I found myself sitting on a long sofa with—these are just *some* of the people who were on that sofa—two co-hosts; Olympic decathlon champion Bruce Jenner; an Italian cookbook author; two large spherical home-improvement contractors wearing matching bright-yellow overalls that would be visible from Mars; two women who wrote a book about something like how to feed a family of 117 people for 23 cents a day; and a complete set of quintuplets.

We did not, to my recollection, discuss the death penalty, but we did change locations a lot; every now and then, for no apparent reason, we'd all jump up and move, herd-like, into another room, where we'd watch somebody show us how to do some Home and Family thing such as baste a turkey. For all I know, that show is still going on. After a while, without being formally excused, I just sort of drifted outside and left, moving briskly past the *Psycho* house.

Yes, the book tour was a lot of effort, but it definitely increased the overall public awareness of my name. I know this because my last appearance was on *The Late Late Show with Tom Snyder*, and at one point, when we came back from a commercial, Tom Snyder, who was not joking, introduced me to the audience as "Chuck Berry." I was not offended; I'm a big fan of Chuck. But if he has a book out, I want a piece of the royalties.

Let's Get Physical

I turned 50, which is really not so old. A lot of very famous people accomplished great things after 50. For example, it was during the post-50 phase of his life that the brilliant physicist Albert Einstein produced the vast majority of his drool.

But still, when you're 50, you're definitely "getting up there," so I decided I'd better go in for my annual physical examination, which is something I do approximately every seven to nine years. I keep my physicals spaced out because my doctor, Curt, who is ordinarily a terrific guy, has a tendency to put on a scary rubber glove and make sudden lunges at my personal region.

Also Curt has some ladies who work with him—and again, these are charming people—who belong to some kind of Druid-style cult that has very strict beliefs under which they are not allowed to let you leave the office with any of your blood. They get you in a chair and distract you with charming conversation while they subtly take your arm and insert a needle attached to a long tube that goes outside to a 50,000-gallon tanker truck with a big sign that says "BLOOD." When they're done draining you, they don't even have to open the door to let you out; they just slide you under it.

Somehow I got through my physical OK. But then, about a week later, Curt was working late one night at his office—perhaps going through the Official Catalog of Supplies for Doctor's Offices, which lists needles in sizes ranging all the way from Extra Large to Harpoon, as well as an extensive selection of pre-1992 magazines with the last page of every article torn out—and he happened to glance up at his framed copy of the Hippocratic oath. This is an oath that is named after an ancient Greek philosopher, Aristotle, who is considered the Father of Medicine because he invented the following phrases, without which modern medical care would be impossible:

—"Do you have insurance?"
—"We're going to have to run some tests."
—"You may experience some discomfort."
—"We're going to have to run some more tests."
—"The tests were inconclusive."

Anyway, Curt was looking at the Hippocratic oath, which all doctors are required to take, and he noticed the sentence that says:

"And I swear by my Lexus that if a person comes into my office for any reason, whether it be for a physical examination or simply to deliver the mail, I will find something medically wrong with that person."

And so Curt, realizing that if he let me get out of my physical scot-free, burly agents of the American Medical Association Ethics Unit would come and yank his stethoscope right out of his ears, called me and told me that the cholesterol level in my blood was a little high. I tried to argue that this was no longer my problem, since all my blood was in the possession of the Druid ladies, but Curt insisted that I had to change my dietary habits.

To help me do this, Curt sent me some informative medical pamphlets that explain to the layperson, via cartoons, what cholesterol is. Technically, it is a little blob-shaped guy with buggy eyes and a big nose who goes running through your blood vessel, which is a tube going to your heart, which can be seen smiling in the background. Sometimes the blob guy gets stuck, causing him to get a grumpy expression and have a balloon come out of his mouth saying, "I'M STUCK." If too many cholesterols get stuck, your blood vessel looks like a New York subway train at rush hour, and your heart gets a sad face, and surgeons have to go in there with a medical device originally developed by Roto-Rooter.

To prevent this from happening, you need to be very careful about your diet, as follows:

FOOD GROUPS YOU CANNOT EAT: Meat, milk, cheese, butter, desserts, processed foods, fried foods, foods with skins, restaurant foods, foods your mom made, foods from packages, foods shown in commercials, foods containing flavor, foods being carried around on trays at wedding receptions, appetizers, snacks, munchies, breakfast, lunch, dinner, take-out, drive-thru, piña coladas, any food with a phrase such as "GOOD LUCK HERB!" written on it in frosting.

FOOD GROUPS YOU CAN EAT: Water (unsweetened), lowfat celery, wood chips.

This diet has been difficult for me to follow. The worst part has been giving up cheese. I love cheese. I'm the kind of person who, merely while rummaging through the refrigerator to see what else is available, can easily gnaw his way through a hunk of cheddar the size of the late Sonny Liston. But I've been pretty good so far, and I'm hoping that my blood cholesterol will be a lot lower, if I ever develop blood again. Curt wants me to come back in and have it checked. He'll never take me alive.

My Final Answer Is ... Go Back to Your Spaceship, Regis

REGIS PHILBIN: Welcome to Who Wants to Be a Millionaire, the dramatic hit quiz show that has all America on the edge of its seat wondering how, exactly, I became famous in the first place. Let's get started with some irritating theme music!

MUSIC: BOM BOM BOM BOMMM!

REGIS: To select our first contestant, we're going to ask our 10 finalists to rank these four things in the order of how much you would not want to have them inserted deep into your ear: (A) A lima bean; (B) A spider; (C) A harmonica; (D) Rosie O'Donnell.

MUSIC: DEEDEEDEEDEEDEEDEE

FINALISTS (shouting over the music): Did you say "ear" or "rear"?

REGIS: Too late! The correct answer is: "(E) It depends on what kind of spider." Our winner is . . . Walter Gweemble of Toledo, Ohio! Come on out here, Walter!

(Walter runs out and shakes hands violently with Regis.)

REGIS: So Walter, tell us about yourself.

WALTER: Well, Regis, I'm . . .

REGIS: Nobody cares, Walter. What loved one have you brought along so that we can heighten the drama by showing his or her reaction as tension mounts?

WALTER: Regis, I brought my dog, Boomer.

(Boomer wags his tail.)

REGIS: OK! Let's play for a MILLION DOLLARS!

MUSIC: DUMDUMDUMDUMDUMDUM!

REGIS: Here we go. For $100, which of the following letters is NOT really a letter? (A) "A"; (B) "B"; (C) "C"; or (D) The Grand Canyon.

MUSIC: AAAAAAAAAAAOOOOOOO

(Walter frowns with deep concentration.)

MUSIC: OOOOOOOOEEEEEEEEEE

REGIS: God, this is dramatic, isn't it?

(The reaction camera shows Boomer, who is engaged in an act of personal hygiene.)

MUSIC: OOOOOOOOAAAAAAAAAAA

WALTER: Regis, I am just not sure what the answer is. But I am really getting off on calling you Regis, Regis.

REGIS: As you know, Walter, you have three lifelines: You can poll the audience; you can make a phone call; or you can have me shout the correct answer out loud, like this: "IT'S 'D,' YOU MORON!"

WALTER: Regis, I'm going to call my mother.

REGIS: We're getting her on the line now. (Sound of phone ringing.)

WALTER'S MOTHER: Hello?

REGIS: Mrs. Gweemble, this is Regis Philbin, with ABC's *Who Wants to Be a Millionaire!*

WALTER'S MOTHER: I told you damn people a million times, we don't want MCI.

WALTER: Mom! It's me! Walter!

WALTER'S MOTHER: Walter?

WALTER: Yes!

WALTER'S MOTHER: You call your mother DURING THE X-FILES?? *(click)*

WALTER: Mom?

REGIS: Walter, please give your final answer, so I can

ask you if your final answer is in fact your final answer. I get paid $25,000 for every time I say "final answer."

MUSIC: OOOOOOOOOEEEEEEEEEE

WALTER: Gosh, Regis, I just don't . . . (He looks over at Boomer, who is drawing a "D" on the floor with his paw.) Regis, I'm going to say . . . "D."

REGIS: Is that your final answer? Final answer? Final answer?

WALTER: Regis, yes.

REGIS: "D" is correct! You've won $100!

MUSIC: BOM BOM BOM BA-DOMMMMM

(Walter collapses. The audience cheers wildly. Boomer makes the Weewee of Triumph on the studio floor.)

REGIS: Whew! Talk about drama! Only 14 more questions to go for a MILLION DOLLARS! Are you nervous, Walter?

WALTER: Well, Regis, I . . .

REGIS: Shut up. Your next question, for $200, is: How many legs are there on a standard cow? (A) None; (B) One; (C) More than one; (D) The Grand Canyon.

MUSIC: OOOOOOOOOEEEEEEEEE

REMOTE CONTROL: Click.

Rubber-Band Man

If you are a regular reader of this column, you know that I make it my business to report on Stuff That Guys Do.

A good example is the sport of snowplow hockey, in which guys driving trucks use their snowplow blades to knock a bowling ball past trucks driven by opposing guys. This is not to be confused with car bowling, in which guys in low-flying airplanes try to drop bowling balls onto junked cars. I've also reported on guys going off a ski jump in a canoe, and on guys trying to build a huge modernized version of a catapult-like medieval war weapon and then using it to hurl a Buick 200 yards.

These are guy activities. These are activities that, when you describe them to a group containing both males and females, provoke two very different reactions:

MALE REACTION: "Cool!"
FEMALE REACTION: "*Why?*"

The answer, of course, is: Because guys like to do stuff. This explains both the Space Shuttle and mailbox vandalism.

Today I want to report on another inspiring example of guys doing stuff. There is a guy in Van Nuys (rhymes with "guys"), California, who is planning, one day soon, to roll down an airport runway and become the first human in recorded history to take off in an airplane that is powered by a rubber band.

I am not making this up. I have met this guy, a 44-year-old stunt pilot whose name happens to be George Heaven. I have also seen his plane, which he designed, and which is called the Rubber Bandit. Do you remember the little rubber-band planes that you used to assemble from pieces of balsa? This plane looks a lot like those, except that it's 33 feet long, with a wingspan of 71 feet and an 18-foot-long propeller. The body is made from high-tech, super-lightweight carbon fiber, so it weighs only 220 pounds without the rubber band, which weighs 90 pounds.

This is not your ordinary rubber band such as you would steal from the supply cabinet at your office. This is made from a continuous strand of rubber that is a quarter inch wide and 3½ miles long; if you stretched it out, it would extend for 24 miles, which means that—to put this in scientific terms—if you shot it at some-body, it would sting like a mother.

The rubber band has been folded back over itself 400 times, so now it forms a fat, 25-foot-long python-like rubber snake on the hangar floor at the Van Nuys Airport. When the big day comes, a winch will wind the rubber band 600 to 800 times, and everybody involved will be very, very careful. You have to watch your step when dealing with your large-caliber rubber bands. I know this from personal experience, because one time a friend of mine named Bill Rose, who is a professional editor at *The Miami Herald* and who likes to shoot rub-ber bands at people, took time out from his busy jour-nalism schedule to construct what he called the Nuclear Rubber Band, which was 300 rubber bands attached together end to end.

One morning in *The Miami Herald* newsroom, I

helped Bill test-fire the Nuclear Rubber Band. I hooked one end over my thumb, and Bill stretched the other end back, back, back, maybe 75 feet. Then he let go. It was an amazing sight to see this whizzing, blurred blob come hurtling through the air, passing me at a high rate of speed and then shooting WAYYYY across the room, where it scored a direct bull's-eye hit smack dab on a fairly personal region of a professional reporter named Jane.

Jane, if you're reading this, let me just say, by way of sincere personal apology, that it was Bill's fault.

The thing is, Bill's rubber band was *nothing* compared with the one that will power George Heaven's Rubber Bandit. If that one were to snap when fully wound, in the words of Rubber Bandit crew chief Tom Beardsley, "it has the potential to kill someone."

Then there is the whole question of what will happen if the Rubber Bandit—with Heaven sitting on a tiny seat hanging below the fuselage, between the wheels— actually takes off. I keep thinking about all the balsa model planes I had when I was a boy. I'd wind the propeller until my finger was sore, then I'd set the plane down on the street, let the prop go, and watch as the plane surged forward, became airborne, and then— guided by some unerring homing instinct that balsa apparently possesses—crashed into the nearest available object and broke into small pieces.

I discussed this with Heaven, who nodded the nod of a man who has heard it all many times. He told me he was not worried at all.

"You're out of your mind," I said.

"I know it," he said.

So there you have it: A Guy on a Mission. Heaven (who looks and sounds a little like the late Robert Mitchum, although he denies this) hopes to make his historic flight around the end of this month. He's trying to raise money so that he and his crew can finish the Rubber Bandit. Naturally you are wondering if he has approached the Trojan condom company about a sponsorship; the answer is yes, he did, and—incredibly—Trojan turned him down.

But he and his volunteers have been working on this project for two years, and I don't think they're going to quit. So keep an eye out for news on the Rubber Bandit. If you live near Van Nuys, you should also keep an ear out, and if you hear a really loud twanging sound, duck.

From Now On, Let Women Kill
Their Own Spiders

From time to time I receive letters from a certain group of individuals that I will describe, for want of a better term, as "women." I have such a letter here, from a Susie Walker of North Augusta, South Carolina, who asks the following question:

"Why do men open a drawer and say, 'Where is the spatula?' instead of, you know, looking for it?"

This question expresses a commonly held (by women) negative stereotype about guys of the male gender, which is that they cannot find things around the house, especially things in the kitchen. Many women believe that if you want to hide something from a man, all you have to do is put it in plain sight in the refrigerator, and he will never, ever find it, as evidenced by the fact that a man can open a refrigerator containing 463 pounds of assorted meats, poultry, cold cuts, condiments, vegetables, frozen dinners, snack foods, desserts, etc., and ask, with no irony whatsoever, "Do we have anything to eat?"

Now I could respond to this stereotype in a snide manner by making generalizations about women. I could ask, for example, how come your average woman prepares for virtually every upcoming event in her life, including dental appointments, by buying new shoes, even if she already owns as many pairs as the entire Riverdance

15

troupe. I could point out that, if there were no women, there would be no such thing as Leonardo DiCaprio. I could ask why a woman would walk up to a perfectly innocent man who is minding his own business watching basketball and demand to know if a certain pair of pants makes her butt look too big, and then, no matter what he answers, get mad at him. I could ask why, according to the best scientific estimates, 93 percent of the nation's severely limited bathroom-storage space is taken up by decades-old, mostly empty tubes labeled "moisturizer." I could point out that, to judge from the covers of countless women's magazines, the two topics most interesting to women are (1) Why men are all disgusting pigs, and (2) How to attract men.

Yes, I could raise these issues in response to the question asked by Susie Walker of North Augusta, South Carolina, regarding the man who was asking where the spatula was. I could even ask WHY this particular man might be looking for the spatula. Could it be that he needs a spatula to kill a spider, because, while he was innocently watching basketball and minding his own business, a member of another major gender—a gender that refuses to personally kill spiders but wants them all dead—DEMANDED that he kill the spider, which nine times out of ten turns out to be a male spider that was minding its own business? Do you realize how many men arrive in hospital emergency rooms every year, sometimes still gripping their spatulas, suffering from painful spider-inflicted injuries? I don't have the exact statistics right here, but I bet they are chilling.

As I say, I could raise these issues and resort to the kind of negativity indulged in by Susie Walker of North Augusta, South Carolina. But I choose not to. I choose, instead, to address her question seriously, in hopes that, by improving the communication between the genders, all human beings—both men and women, together—will come to a better understanding of how dense women can be sometimes.

I say this because there is an excellent reason why a man would open the spatula drawer and, without looking for the spatula, ask where the spatula is: The man does not have TIME to look for the spatula. Why? Because he is busy thinking. Men are almost always thinking. When you look at a man who appears to be merely scratching himself, rest assured that inside his head, his brain is humming like a high-powered computer, processing millions of pieces of information and producing important insights such as, "This feels good!"

We should be grateful that men think so much, because over the years they have thought up countless inventions that have made life better for all people, everywhere. The shot clock in basketball is one example. Another one is underwear-eating bacteria. I found out about this thanks to the many alert readers who sent me an article from *New Scientist* magazine stating that Russian scientists—and you KNOW these are guy scientists—are trying to solve the problem of waste disposal aboard spacecraft, by "designing a cocktail of bacteria to digest astronauts' cotton and paper underpants." Is that great, or what? I am picturing a utopian future wherein, when a man's briefs get dirty, they will simply dissolve from his body, thereby freeing him from the chore of dealing with his soiled underwear via the labor-intensive, time-consuming method he now uses, namely, dropping them on the floor.

I'm not saying that guys have solved all the world's problems. I'm just saying that there ARE solutions out there, and if, instead of harping endlessly about spatulas, we allow guys to use their mental talents to look for these solutions, in time, they will find them. Unless they are in the refrigerator.

Here's Mud in Your Eye

Recently I spent several days touring the California wine country, and I must say that it was a wonderful experience that I will remember until long after I get this mud out of my ears.

I'll explain the mud in a moment, but first I should explain that the wine country is an area near San Francisco that is abundantly blessed with the crucial natural ingredient that you need to have a successful wine country: tourists. There are thousands and thousands of them, forming a dense continuous stream of rental cars creeping up and down the Napa Valley, where you apparently cannot be a legal resident unless you own a winery named after yourself. Roughly every 45 feet you pass a sign that says something like "The Earl A. Frebblemunster And His Sons Earl Jr. And Bud, But Not Fred, Who Went Into The Insurance Business, Winery."

When you see a winery that you like, you go inside for wine-related activities, which are mainly (1) tasting wine, and (2) trying to adopt thoughtful facial expressions so as to appear as though you have some clue as to what you are tasting. Some wineries also give guided tours wherein they show you how wine is made. The process starts with the grapes, which ripen on vines under the watchful eyes of the head wine person (or "poisson de la tête") until exactly the right moment, at which point

19

they form a huge swarm and follow the queen to the new hive location.

No, wait, I'm thinking of bees. When the grapes are ripe, they're harvested and stomped on barefoot by skilled stompers until they (the grapes) form a pulpy mass (called the "fromage") which is then discarded. Then the head wine person drives to the supermarket and buys some nice hygienic bunches of unstomped grapes, which are placed in containers with yeast—a small but sexually active fungus—and together they form wine.

The wine is then bottled and transported to the Pretentious Phrase Room, where professional wine snots perform the most critical part of the whole operation: thinking of ways to make fermented grape juice sound more complex than nuclear physics. For example, at one winery I sampled a Pinot Noir (from the French words "pinot," meaning "type of," and "noir," meaning "wine") and they handed me a sheet of paper giving many facts about the wine, including something called the "Average Brix at Harvest"; the pH of the grapes; a detailed discussion of the fermentation (among other things, it was "malolactic"); the type of barrels used for aging ("100 percent French tight-grained oak from the Vosges and Allier forests"); the type of filtration (it was "a light egg-white fining"); and of course the actual nature of the wine itself, which is described—and this is only part of the description—as having "classical Burgundian aromas of earth, bark, and mushrooms; dried leaves, cherries; subtle hints of spice and French oak"; and of course the flavor of "blackberry, allspice, cloves, vanilla with nuances of plums and toast."

Yes! Nuances of toast! I bet they exchanged high fives in the Pretentious Phrase Room when they came up with that one!

At another winery, I stood next to some young men—

they couldn't have been older than 22—who were tasting wine and making serious facial expressions and asking a winery employee questions such as: "Was '93 a good year for the Cabernets?" I wanted to shake them and shout, "What's WRONG with you!? When I was your age, I was drinking Sunshine Premium brand beer (motto: 'Made From Ingredients') at $2.39 a CASE!"

Needless to say, these young men also had cigars. You have to worry about where this nation is headed.

Anyway, the other major tourist thing to do in wine country is to go to a town called Calistoga and take a mud bath, which is an activity that I believe would be popular only in an area where people have been drinking wine. My wife and I took one at a combination spa and motel, where we were met by a woman who said, I swear, "Hi, I'm Marcie, and I'll be your mud attendant."

Marcie led us into a room containing two large tubs filled to the brim with what smelled like cow poop heated to 104 degrees. We paid good money to be allowed to climb into these things and lie there sweating like professional wrestlers for 15 minutes. Marcie—who later admitted that she had done this only once herself—said it was supposed to get rid of our bodily toxins, but my feeling is that from now on, if I have to choose between toxins and hot cow poop, I'm going with the toxins.

But I have to say that once I got out of the mud, I felt a great deal better than when I was in the mud, and I am confident that one day, if I take enough showers, people will stop edging away from me on the elevator. So let me just close by saying that, although I have made some fun of the wine-country experience here, I really do feel, in all sincerity, that "Pinot Noir and His Nuances of Toast" would be a good name for a band.

Eye of the Beholder

Like many members of the uncultured, Cheez-It-consuming public, I am not good at grasping modern art. I'm the type of person who will stand in front of a certified modern masterpiece painting that looks, to the layperson, like a big black square, and quietly think: "Maybe the actual painting is on the other side."

I especially have a problem with modernistic sculptures, the kind where you, the layperson, cannot be sure whether you're looking at a work of art or a crashed alien spacecraft. My definition of a good sculpture is "a sculpture that looks at least vaguely like something." I'm talking about a sculpture like Michelangelo's *David*. You look at that, and there is no doubt about what the artist's message is. It is: "Here's a naked man the size of an oil derrick."

I bring this topic up because of an interesting incident that occurred recently in Miami. When people ask me, "Dave, why do you choose voluntarily to live in Miami?" I answer, "Because interesting incidents are always occurring here." For example, just recently (DIGRESSION ALERT) federal agents here arrested two men on charges of attempting to illegally sell weapons.

"Big deal!" you are saying. "Federal agents in many cities regularly arrest people for illegally selling weapons!"

Right. But these were *nuclear* weapons. I swear I am not making this up. The two suspects are Lithuanian nationals; they were allegedly working on a deal to sell undercover agents some Russian-made tactical nuclear weapons.

Call me a Nervous Nellie, but I am concerned about the sale of nuclear arms in my general neighborhood. I say this because of the popular Miami tradition, which I am also not making up, of celebrating festive occasions by discharging weapons into the air. I am picturing a scenario wherein some Miami guy chugs one too many bottles of Cold Duck at his New Year's party, and when the clock strikes midnight, he staggers over to the closet where he keeps his tactical nuclear weapon—which he told his wife he was buying strictly for personal protection—and he says to himself, "I wonder how THAT baby would sound!"

But my point (END OF DIGRESSION ALERT) is that Miami tends to have these interesting incidents, and one of them occurred a little while ago when Dade County purchased an office building from the city of Miami. The problem was that, squatting in an area that the county wanted to convert into office space, there was a large ugly wad of metal, set into the concrete. So the county sent construction workers with heavy equipment to rip out the wad, which was then going to be destroyed.

But guess what? Correct! It turns out that this was NOT an ugly wad. It was art! Specifically, it was Public Art, defined as "art that is purchased by experts who are not spending their own personal money." The money of course comes from the taxpayers, who are not allowed to spend this money themselves because (1) they probably wouldn't buy art, and (2) if they did, there is no way they would buy the crashed-spaceship style of art that the experts usually select for them.

The Miami wad is in fact a sculpture by the famous Italian sculptor Pomodoro (like most famous artists, he is not referred to by his first name, although I like to think it's "Bud"). This sculpture cost the taxpayers $80,000, which makes it an important work of art. In dollar terms, it is 3,200 times as important as a painting of dogs playing poker, and more than 5,000 times as important as a velveteen Elvis.

Fortunately, before the sculpture was destroyed, the error was discovered, and the Pomodoro was moved to another city office building, where it sits next to the parking garage, providing great pleasure to the many taxpayers who come to admire it.

I am kidding, of course. On the day I went to see it, the sculpture was, like so many pieces of modern taxpayer-purchased public art, being totally ignored by the actual taxpaying public, possibly because it looks—and I say this with all due artistic respect for Bud—like an abandoned air compressor.

So here's what I think: I think there should be a law

requiring that all public art be marked with a large sign stating something like: "NOTICE! THIS IS A PIECE OF ART! THE PUBLIC SHOULD ENJOY IT TO THE TUNE OF 80,000 CLAMS!"

Also, if there happens to be an abandoned air compressor nearby, it should have a sign that says: "NOTICE! THIS IS NOT ART!" so the public does not waste time enjoying the wrong thing. The public should enjoy what the experts have decided the public should enjoy. That's the system we use in this country, and we're going to stick with it. At least until the public acquires missiles.

Fore!

You've surely noticed that a big golf craze is sweeping the nation, as aging Baby Boomers discover the benefits of participating in a sport where the most physically demanding activity is ordering putters by mail.

It has reached the point where, if you don't play golf, your career can suffer. I know mine has. In my newspaper office, the two senior editors—let's call them "Tom Shroder" and "Bill Rose"—regularly go off together during business hours to play golf. I'm sure that while they're out on the "links" whacking their "bogeys," they discuss important business matters and formulate newspaper policies in conversations like this:

•

TOM: Bill, before I attempt to "shank" this "birdie," I'd like to know your "gut feeling" on the use of quotation marks in the newspaper.
BILL: Tom, I feel they are overused.
TOM: I agree. Let's formulate a policy on that.
BILL: And then let's try on evening gowns.
TOM: Yes! We'll accessorize with brooches!

I'm not saying "Tom" and "Bill" discuss exactly these topics. I'm merely saying that, because I don't play golf, I don't know WHAT they discuss, and so I'm "out of the loop." Perhaps you're "in the same boat." Perhaps you'd like to learn about golf, so that when your colleagues talk about it, you can join in and be "one of the persons." That's why today's topic is Basic Questions About Golf, starting with the question that beginners ask most often:

Q. Has anybody ever used a 9-iron to kill emus?

A. Alert reader Marjorie Dishron sent me a fascinating column written last February by Ron Henry Strait, outdoor writer for *The San Antonio Express-News*; the column concerns a man named Wes Linthicum, who heads an informal group called the Texas Christian Hunters Association, which each year feeds the homeless using donated meat. An area emu farmer offered to give the group a bunch of emus, which are very large, ostrich-like birds. The problem was that the birds were alive, and, as the old folk saying goes, "You can't feed large ostrich-like birds to the homeless if they [the birds] are walking around." The members of the Texas Christian Hunters Association didn't have guns with them, and nobody wanted to strangle the emus manually. According to the column, the problem was solved when:

"... someone recalled that emus have a tendency to closely examine an object that is dropped on the ground. That's when Linthicum got out his 9-iron ..."

I called Linthicum, and he told me, after some hemming and hawing, that although the story he'd related to columnist Strait was essentially correct, the golf-club part was not 100 percent accurate in the sense of being true. Linthicum also made these points: (1) If you are ever offered a gift of live emus, you would be wise to turn it down, because "those things have feet like something out of *Jurassic Park*"; (2) If it gets printed in the newspaper that you dispatched emus with a 9-iron, even for a good cause, you're going to hear from some extremely angry animal-rights people; and (3) If a person, for whatever reason, did have to dispatch an emu with a golfing implement, it would make more sense to use a wood than an iron.

Speaking of *Jurassic Park*, another question often asked by beginning golfers is:

Q. What happens if a snake eats my balls?

A. Don't worry! The snake will be fine, provided that it gets proper medical care. I base this statement on an article from the July 5, 1996, Harrisburg (Pennsylvania) *Patriot-News*, written by Danielle Hollister and alertly sent in by Dave Barrows, headlined SURGERY GETS SNAKE UP TO PAR. The story states that Sandy and Jeff Paul, who raise chickens, sometimes "put golf balls in their hens' nests to encourage the hens to stay put and lay eggs." One day they noticed a five-foot rat snake near their home with three distinct lumps in its middle, and they realized that the snake had swallowed their golf balls. So they grabbed their 9-iron and . . .

No, seriously, according to the *Patriot-News* article, the Pauls contacted a veterinarian, who successfully removed the golf balls. The snake, which the Pauls named "Spalding," came through the operation OK and has been accepted to law school.

No, I'm kidding about that last part. But I'm not kidding about our final common golf question, which is:

Q. If I do not wish to stand around on a golf course listening to a bunch of business clients drone on about their "mulligans," can I hire somebody to play golf with them for me?

A. Yes! Alert dentist Steve Carstensen sent me a flyer for a new Seattle outfit called Golf In Action ("We'll Play for You When You Can't"). The idea is, you pay a golfer to take your clients out and play with them, thereby (to quote the flyer) "giving you the freedom to continue your important daily business needs."

I called Golf In Action and spoke with the founder, Sheila Locke, who told me that her idea has gotten a good public response, although a lot of the calls are from people who want to join her staff and get paid to play golf.

Me, I love the idea of paying somebody to play golf with your clients, and I'm thinking: Why not take it further? Why not pay somebody to have meetings with your clients, and take your clients to dinner, and smoke cigars and drink brandy with your clients, and then throw up on your clients' shoes because you hate brandy and cigars? This company could be called: Businesspersons In Action.

So those are your golf basics. Good luck out on the "links," and be sure to say "hi" to my editors, "Tom" and "Bill," who will be easy to spot because they get stuck in the sand traps with those high heels.

Fore! II

I imagine you sports fans are dying to learn the results of my golf tournament.

That is correct: I have a golf tournament. It used to be that you had to be a major star such as a Bob Hope or a Moammar Gadhafi to have one, but now anybody can. It has reached the point where, if you apply for a credit card, the first two blanks on the application are "Your Name" and "Name of Your Golf Tournament."

Mine is "The Dave Barry Classic," and it attempts to raise money for the American Red Cross. I'm a fan of the Red Cross, because after Hurricane Andrew devastated South Florida, the Red Cross provided us with the one thing we most desperately needed: showers. This was a godsend, because after a few days without plumbing, we all smelled like Eau de Athletic Supporter.

And so when the local Red Cross chapter asked me if I'd host a golf tournament, my answer, without one instant of hesitation, was: "I don't play golf." This is true. I don't have anything *against* golf; it's just that, if I'm going to play a sport, I want one that provides more aerobic benefits, such as "Rock, Paper, Scissors."

But I told the Red Cross people I'd host the tournament anyway, because I sincerely believe in "giving something back" to the community. Plus they said there would be beer.

The Dave Barry Classic was held at Doral Park, which is a residential golfing community catering to people who enjoy combining the pleasure of living in attractive homes with the pleasure of never knowing exactly when a small, hard, white sphere will penetrate your recreation room traveling upward of 140 miles per hour. This happens routinely because golfers, despite the fact that they are using expensive, modern golf clubs made from space-age materials and engineered to tolerances of thousandths of an inch, have absolutely no idea what the golf ball is going to do once they hit it.

I say this after spending a day observing the golfers in my tournament. These were mostly middle-aged business guys who had come out because they truly believe in the ideals of the Red Cross, especially the ideal of holding a golf tournament on a Friday afternoon.

"I would love to stay in the office wearing a tie and talking on the phone with boring people I dislike," they probably told their business associates, "but I have an obligation to the Red Cross."

In addition to the business guys, we had some big celebrities on hand. I do not mean "big" in the sense of "famous"; I mean "big" as in "larger than your junior high school." For example, one celebrity was Charles "Gator" Bennett, a former defensive lineperson with the Miami Dolphins. At one point "Gator" playfully put his arm, which is the size of Keanu Reeves, around my neck, thereby playfully shutting down my trachea for what at the time seemed like an eternity, but which in fact, as I look back on it, was probably only about 45 minutes. This is exactly why I hated gym class. I was afraid that "Gator" would decide to snap me with a towel, and I would never walk again.

Not that I felt much safer on the golf course. For one thing, there were the killer ducks. The Doral Park course has a large colony of ducks that, after years of eating food dropped by golfers, have become large and aggressive. If you stop your golf cart, they surround you, dozens of them, pretty much demanding that you give them something to eat.

"We can peck you to death," is their unmistakable message, "and the authorities will do nothing to us, because we are ducks."

More than once I found myself stomping on the accelerator and rocketing away at top golf-cart speed ("mosey"), with a herd of irate ducks waddling after me, like a terrifying scene from a Steven Spielberg movie called *Jurassic Duck*.

But the scariest phenomenon on the golf course, as I noted earlier, is the golfers. Basically, every time they hit the ball, they go through two distinct phases:

PHASE ONE—They are a foursome of serious, middle-aged accountants, bankers, lawyers, doctors, etc., gathering around a golf ball, studying it intensely, as though it were an unexploded terrorist bomb. Then one of them takes a club, stands over the ball, waggles his butt around, hauls off and hits the ball, which leads to . . .

PHASE TWO—All four golfers instantly transform into lunatics, gyrating their bodies and screaming contradictory instructions at the ball ("STAY UP!" "GET DOWN!" "STAY DOWN!" "GET UP!"). They sound like the deranged homeless people you sometimes see shouting on city streets, the difference being that, at least some of the time, somebody might be listening to the deranged homeless people, whereas the ball never listens to the golfers. It goes wherever it wants, laughing the laugh of the truly carefree.

So what with the golfers and "Gator" and the gangsta ducks, it was a scary day out there on the "links." But I'm pleased to report that we got through The Dave Barry Classic without any unnecessary deaths, although as of this morning there still were several tee shots that had not yet returned to Earth, so if you live within 250 miles of Miami, you are advised to cower under your bed until further notice.

And if, God forbid, something bad should happen, you may rest assured that the Red Cross will be there for you.

Another Road Hog
with Too Much Oink

If there's one thing this nation needs, it's bigger cars. That's why I'm excited that Ford is coming out with a new mound o' metal that will offer consumers even more total road-squatting mass than the current leader in the humongous-car category, the popular Chevrolet Suburban Subdivision—the first passenger automobile designed to be, right off the assembly line, visible from the Moon.

I don't know what the new Ford will be called. Probably something like the "Ford Untamed Wilderness Adventure." In the TV commercials, it will be shown splashing through rivers, charging up rocky mountainsides, swinging on vines, diving off cliffs, racing through the surf, and fighting giant sharks hundreds of feet beneath the ocean surface—all the daredevil things that cars do in Sport Utility Vehicle Commercial World, where nobody ever drives on an actual road. In fact, the interstate highways in Sport Utility Vehicle Commercial World, having been abandoned by humans, are teeming with deer, squirrels, birds, and other wildlife species that have fled from the forest to avoid being run over by nature-seekers in multi-ton vehicles barreling through the underbrush at 50 miles per hour.

In the real world, of course, nobody drives Sport Utility Vehicles in the forest, because when you have paid upward of $40,000 for a transportation investment, the last thing you want is squirrels pooping on it. No, if you want a practical "off-road" vehicle, you get yourself a 1973 American Motors Gremlin, which combines the advantage of not being worth worrying about with the advantage of being so ugly that poisonous snakes flee from it in terror.

In the real world, what people mainly do with their Sport Utility Vehicles, as far as I can tell, is try to maneuver them into and out of parking spaces. I base this statement on my local supermarket, where many of the upscale patrons drive Chevrolet Subdivisions. I've noticed that these people often purchase just a couple of items—maybe a bottle of diet water and a two-ounce package of low-fat dried carrot shreds—which they put into the back of their Subdivisions, which have approximately the same cargo capacity, in cubic feet, as Finland. This means there is plenty of room left over back there in case, on the way home, these people decide to pick up something else, such as a herd of bison.

Then comes the scary part: getting the Subdivision out of the parking space. This is a challenge, because the driver apparently cannot, while sitting in the driver's seat, see all the way to either end of the vehicle. I drive a compact car, and on a number of occasions I have found myself trapped behind a Subdivision backing directly toward me, its massive metal butt looming high over my head, making me feel like a Tokyo pedestrian looking up at Godzilla.

I've tried honking my horn, but the Subdivision drivers can't hear me, because they're always talking on cellular phones the size of Chiclets ("The Bigger Your Car, the Smaller Your Phone," that is their motto). I don't know who they're talking to. Maybe they're negotiating with their bison suppliers. Or maybe they're trying to contact somebody in the same area code as the rear ends of their cars, so they can find out what's going on back there. All I know is, I'm thinking of carrying marine flares, so I can fire them into the air as a warning to Subdivision drivers that they're about to run me over. Although frankly I'm not sure they'd care if they did. A big reason why they bought a Sport Utility Vehicle is "safety," in the sense of, "you, personally, will be safe, although every now and then you may have to clean the remains of other motorists out of your wheel wells."

Anyway, now we have the new Ford, which will be *even larger* than the Subdivision, which I imagine means it will have separate decks for the various classes of passengers, and possibly, way up in front by the hood ornament, Leonardo DiCaprio showing Kate Winslet how to fly. I can't wait until one of these babies wheels into my supermarket parking lot. Other motorists and pedestrians will try to flee in terror, but they'll be sucked in by the Ford's powerful gravitational field and become stuck to its massive sides like so many refrigerator magnets. They won't be noticed, however, by the Ford's driver, who will be busy whacking at the side of his or her head, trying to dislodge his or her new cell phone, which is the size of a single grain of rice and has fallen deep into his or her ear canal.

And it will not stop there. This is America, darn it, and Chevrolet is not about to just sit by and watch Ford walk away with the coveted title of Least Sane Motor Vehicle. No, cars will keep getting bigger: I see a time, not too far from now, when upscale suburbanites will haul their overdue movies back to the video-rental store in full-size, 18-wheel tractor-trailers with names like The Vagabond.

It will be a proud time for all Americans, a time for us to cheer for our country. We should cheer loud, because we'll be hard to hear, inside the wheel wells.

Bon Appétit

Today's topic is: The Art of Cooking

Cooking was invented in prehistoric times, when a primitive tribe had a lucky accident. The tribe had killed an animal and was going to eat it raw, when a tribe member named Woog tripped and dropped it into the fire. At first the other tribe members were angry at Woog, but then, as the aroma of burning meat filled the air, they had an idea. So they ate Woog raw.

Yes, cooking can be hazardous. I learned this lesson from a dramatic true incident that occurred in my childhood. My family was at home, waiting for company to arrive; my mom was cooking one of her specialties, creamed chipped beef, in a double boiler. There was a knock at the door, and we all went to the living room to greet our company, which was fortunate because at exactly the instant we opened the door, the double boiler exploded violently, sending what seemed like thousands of gallons of creamed chipped beef flying in all directions with tremendous force. I believe that if there are intelligent beings elsewhere in the universe, one day their astronomers will detect traces of this particular entree spreading out across the cosmos at nearly the speed of light, and they will, by extrapolating backward, calculate that a cataclysmic Big Beef Bang took place on Earth in 1958.

The point is that, as a safety precaution, you should never cook anything, including toast, without wearing a welding helmet. Also you should choose a recipe that is appropriate for the individuals who will be eating it. For example, you do not need to make an elaborate dish if the individuals are dogs. A dog will eat pretty much anything; one major reason why there are no restaurants for dogs is that the customers would eat the menus. So a dog will happily eat the same recipe forever. You can feed a dog "kibble," which is actually compressed dirt, every single day for 13 years, and the dog will consider you to be the greatest cook in world history. It will lick the ground you walk on.

The situation is similar with guys. Guys generally like to find a recipe that works for them and stick with it. For example, I know a sportswriter named Bob who, to my knowledge, has never in his life cooked anything except Stouffer's frozen French bread pizza. This is all he has in his freezer. If he hosted a Thanksgiving dinner, he'd serve a large Stouffer's French bread pizza, stuffed with smaller Stouffer's French bread pizzas. At the Stouffer's factory, they probably have a whole department devoted exclusively to Bob, called "The Department of Bob," which monitors Bob's pizza consumption and has a fleet of loaded resupply trucks ready to roll when he runs low.

If you're not cooking for guys or dogs, you should use a more elaborate "gourmet" type of recipe, which you can find in magazines such as *Bon Appétit* (literal translation: "Chow Down"). The problem here is that the people who are creating these recipes are also snorking down cooking wine by the gallon, and after a while they start making up words. Take "fennel." There is no such thing as "fennel," yet many of your gourmet recipes call for it. Other examples of imaginary ingredients are "shallots," "capers," and "arugula." So what frequently happens when you try to make a gourmet recipe is, you're progressing briskly through the steps, and suddenly you come across an instruction that the gourmet chef obviously dreamed up moments before passing out face-down in the béarnaise sauce, such as "Carmelize eight minced hamouti kleebers into a reduction of blanched free-range whelk corneas."

Thus to be a successful cook, you need to learn how to adapt gourmet recipes to the "real world" by making substitutions. For example, recently I was looking through the December issue of *Bon Appétit*, and I found a recipe called "Sweet Potato Soup with Lobster and Orange Crème Fraîche." I was very interested in making this recipe; the problem was that some of the ingredients, such as "leeks," were obviously imaginary, whereas others, such as lobster, were members of the cockroach family. No problem! I simply looked around my kitchen for appropriate substitute ingredients, and I was able to adapt the *Bon Appétit* recipe to meet my specific needs, as follows:

SWEET POTATO SOUP WITH LOBSTER AND ORANGE CRÈME FRAÎCHE

1. *In a medium room, remove wrappers from eight miniature Three Musketeers bars left over from Halloween.*
2. *Eat bars.*
3. *Feed wrappers to dog.*

With a little ingenuity, you can achieve results very much like this in your own kitchen. I bet that when word of your culinary prowess gets around, people will be flocking to your door! Let's hope they're bringing pizza.

Road Warrior

If you do much driving on our nation's highways, you've probably noticed that, more and more often, bullets are coming through your windshield. This is a common sign of Road Rage, which the opinion-makers in the news media have decided is a serious problem, currently ranking just behind global warming and several points ahead of Asia.

How widespread is Road Rage? To answer that question, researchers for the National Institute of Traffic Safety recently did a study in which they drove on the interstate highway system in a specially equipped observation van. By the third day, they were deliberately running other motorists off the road.

"These people are MORONS!" was their official report.

That is the main cause of Road Rage: the realization that many of your fellow motorists have the same brain structure as a cashew. The most common example, of course, is the motorists who feel a need to drive in the left-hand, or "passing," lane, even though they are going slower than everybody else. Nobody knows why these motorists do this. Maybe they belong to some kind of religious cult that believes the right lane is sacred and must never come in direct contact with tires. Maybe one time, years ago, these motorists happened to be driving in the left lane when their favorite song came on the radio, so they've driven over there ever since, in hopes that the radio will play that song again.

But whatever makes these people drive this way, there's nothing you can do about it. You can honk at them, but it will have no effect. People have been honking at them for years: It's a normal part of their environment. They've decided that, for some mysterious reason, wherever they drive, there is honking. They choose not to ponder this mystery any further, lest they overburden their cashews.

I am very familiar with this problem, because I live and drive in Miami, which proudly bills itself as The Inappropriate-Lane-Driving Capital Of The World, a place where the left lane is thought of not so much as a thoroughfare as a public recreational area, where motorists feel free to stop, hold family reunions, barbecue pigs, play volleyball, etc. Compounding this problem is another common type of Miami motorist, the aggressive young male whose car has a sound system so powerful that the driver must go faster than the speed of sound at all times, because otherwise the nuclear bass notes emanating from his rear speakers will catch up to him and cause his head to explode.

So the tiny minority of us Miami drivers who actually qualify as normal find ourselves constantly being trapped behind people drifting along on the interstate at the speed of diseased livestock, while at the same time we are being tailgated and occasionally bumped from behind by testosterone-deranged youths who got their driver training from watching the space-fighter battle scenes in *Star Wars*. And of course nobody EVER signals or yields, and people are CONSTANTLY cutting us off, and AFTER A WHILE WE START TO FEEL SOME

RAGE, OK? YOU GOT A PROBLEM WITH THAT, MISTER NEWS MEDIA OPINION-MAKER??

In addition to Road Rage, I frequently experience Parking Lot Rage, which occurs when I pull into a crowded supermarket parking lot, and I see people get into their car, clearly ready to leave, so I stop my car and wait for them to vacate the spot, and . . . nothing happens! They just stay there! WHAT THE HELL ARE THEY DOING IN THERE??!! COOKING DINNER???

When I finally get into the supermarket, I often experience Shopping Cart Rage. This is caused by the people—and you just KNOW these are the same people who always drive in the left-hand lane—who routinely manage, by careful placement, to block the entire aisle with a single shopping cart. If we really want to keep illegal immigrants from entering the United States, we should employ Miami residents armed with shopping carts; we'd only need about two dozen to block the entire Mexican border.

What makes the supermarket congestion even worse is that shoppers are taking longer and longer to decide what to buy, because every product in America now comes in an insane number of styles and sizes. For example, I recently went to the supermarket to get orange juice. For just *one brand* of orange juice, Tropicana, I had to decide whether I wanted Original, HomeStyle, Pulp Plus, Double Vitamin C, Grovestand, Calcium, or Old-Fashioned; I also had to decide whether I wanted the 16-ounce, 32-ounce, 64-ounce, 96-ounce, or six-pack size. This is WAY too many product choices. It caused me to experience Way Too Many Product Choices Rage. I would have called Tropicana and complained, but I probably would have wound up experiencing Automated Phone Answering System Rage (". . . For questions about Pulp Plus in the 32-ounce size, press 23. For questions about Pulp Plus in the 64-ounce size, press 24. For questions about . . .").

My point is that there are many causes for rage in our modern world, and if we're going to avoid unnecessary violence, we all need to "keep our cool." So let's try to be more considerate, OK? Otherwise I will kill you.

Weird Science

**Today's topic for young people is: How to Do a School
Science-Fair Project**

So your school is having a science fair! Great! The
science fair has long been a favorite educational tool in
the American school system, and for a good reason:
Your teachers hate you.

Ha ha! No, seriously, although a science fair can seem
like a big "pain," it can help you understand important
scientific principles, such as Newton's First Law of Iner-
tia, which states: "A body at rest will remain at rest until
8:45 P.M. the night before the science-fair project is due,
at which point the body will come rushing to the body's
parents, who are already in their pajamas, and shout,
'I JUST REMEMBERED THE SCIENCE FAIR IS TO-
MORROW AND WE GOTTA GO TO THE STORE
RIGHT NOW!'"

Being driven to the store by pajama-wearing parents at
the last minute is the most important part of any science-
fair project, because your project, to be legal, must have
an Official Science-Fair Display Board. This is a big
white board that you fold into three sections, thus giving it the stability that it needs to collapse instantly
when approached by humans. The international scientific community does not recognize any scientific discovery that does not have an Official Science-Fair Display

Board teetering behind it; many top scientists fail to win the Nobel Prize for exactly this reason.

Once you have returned home and gotten your display board folded into three sections (allow about six hours for this) it's time to start thinking about what kind of project to do. The prize-winning projects are the ones that clearly yet imaginatively demonstrate an interesting scientific principle. So you can forget about winning a prize. What you need is a project that can be done at 1 A.M. using materials found in your house. Ideally, it should also involve a minimum of property damage or death, which is why, on the advice of this newspaper's legal counsel, we are not going to discuss some of our popular project topics from previous years, such as "What Is Inside Plumbing?" and "Flame-Proofing Your Cat."

Whatever topic you select, your project should be divided into three parts: (1) The Hypothesis; (2) The Part That Goes After the Hypothesis; and (3) The Conclusion (this should always be the same as the Hypothesis).

The hypothesis—which comes from the Greek words "hypot," meaning "word," and "hesis," meaning "that I am looking up in the dictionary right now"—is defined as "an unproved theory, proposition, supposition, etc. tentatively accepted to explain certain facts." For example, a good hypothesis for your science-fair project might be: "There is a lot of gravity around." You could prove this via an experiment in which you pick up various household items such as underwear, small appliances, siblings, etc., and observe what happens when you let go of them. Your conclusion would of course be: "There is a lot of gravity around." This would be dramatically illustrated, in your science-fair exhibit, by the fact that your Official Science-Fair Display Board was lying face-down on the floor.

If that project sounds like too much effort, you might consider duplicating the one that my wife swears she did in the seventh grade late on the night before the science fair. It was called "Waves," and it consisted entirely of a baking pan filled with water, and a pencil.

"You swished the pencil around in the water, and it made waves," my wife explained.

I asked her what scientific principle this project demonstrated, and, after thinking about it for a moment, she answered: "The movement of the water."

Impossible though it may sound, I did a project in sixth grade that was even lamer than that. It was called "Phases of the Moon," and it consisted of a small rubber ball that I had darkened half of by scribbling on it with a pen. You were supposed to rotate the ball, thus demonstrating scientifically that the phases of the Moon were caused by, I don't know, ink.

The total elapsed time involved in conceiving of and constructing this project was maybe 10 minutes, of which at least nine were devoted to scribbling. But it still might have been a success had it not been for the fact that some of my fellow students found it amusing to snatch up the Moon and throw it, so that it became sort of a gypsy exhibit, traveling around the Harold C. Crittenden Junior High School gymnasium, landing in and becoming part of other projects, helping to demonstrate magnetism, photosynthesis, etc. So my project ended up being just a sign saying "PHASES OF THE MOON" sitting on an otherwise bare naked table, the scientific implication being that the Moon is a very moody celestial body that sometimes gets in a phase where it just takes off without telling anybody.

Of course if you want to get a good grade, you have to do a project that will impress your teachers. Here's a proven winner:

"HYPOTHESIS—That (Name of Teacher) and (Name of Another Teacher) would prefer that I not distribute the photo I took of them when they were 'chaperoning' our class trip to Epcot Center and they ducked behind the cottage-cheese exhibit in the Amazing World Of Curds."

Depending on the quality of your research, you might get more than a good grade from your teachers: You might get actual money! Yes, science truly can be rewarding. So why wait until the last minute to start your science-fair project? Why not get started immediately on exploring the amazing world of science, without which we would not have modern technology. Television, for example. Let's turn it on right now.

The Tool Man

I was walking through my bedroom on a recent Sunday morning when I suddenly had a feeling that something was wrong. I'm not sure how I knew; perhaps it was a "sixth sense" I've developed after years of home ownership. Or perhaps it was the fact that there was water coming out of the ceiling.

But whatever tipped me off, I knew that I had a potentially serious problem, so I did not waste time. Moving swiftly but without panic, I went into the living room and read the entire sports section of the newspaper, thus giving the problem a chance to go away by itself. This is one of the four recommended methods for dealing with a household problem, the other three being (1) wrapping the problem with duct tape; (2) spraying the problem with a product called "WD-40"; and (3) selling the home, and then telling the new owners, "Hey, it never did that when WE owned it."

Unfortunately, when I went back to the bedroom, the ceiling was still dripping. My wife, Michelle, suggested that maybe there was water sitting on the roof and leaking into the house, but I knew, as an experienced guy of the male gender, that she was wrong. I knew that the problem was the plumbing. It's time that we homeowners accepted the fact that plumbing is a bad idea. Many historians believe that the primary reason why the Roman empire collapsed is that the Romans attempted to install plumbing in it. Suddenly, instead of being ruthless, all-conquering warriors, they became a bunch of guys scurrying around trying to repair leaking viaducts. (Tragically, the Romans did not have "WD-40.")

So I knew that our plumbing had broken, and I also knew why it had chosen that particular morning: We had a houseguest. Plumbing can sense the arrival of a houseguest, and it often responds by leaking or causing toilets to erupt like porcelain volcanoes. And of course our plumbing had waited until Sunday, which meant that the plumber would not come for at least a day, which meant that it was up to me, as a male, to climb up into the attic and do the manly thing that men have had to do as long as men have been men: shine a flashlight around.

"Maybe you should check the roof first," said Michelle. "Maybe there's water sitting up there."

She was fixated on this roof theory. Women can be

like that. I had to explain to her, being as patient as possible considering that I had urgent guy tasks to perform, that she was being an idiot, because THE PROBLEM WAS THE PLUMBING.

So I got my flashlight and climbed up a ladder into the attic, where I was able, thanks to my experience as a homeowner and my natural mechanical sense, to get pieces of insulation deep into my nose. I was not, however, able to locate the source of the leak, because my attic turned out to be a cramped, dark, dirty, mysterious place with pipes and wires running all over the place, and off in the distance—just out of flashlight reach, but I could definitely sense its presence—a tarantula the size of the Reverend Jerry Falwell.

So I came briskly back down the ladder and told Michelle that, to stop the plumbing from leaking, I was going to turn off all the water to the house until the plumber came. Speaking in clipped, efficient, manly sentences, I instructed Michelle to fill containers with water and write a note for the houseguest telling him how to flush his toilet with a bucket.

"Before we do all that," she said, "Maybe you should check the . . ."

"DON'T TELL ME TO CHECK THE ROOF!" I explained. "STOP TALKING ABOUT THE ROOF! THE PROBLEM IS THE PLUMBING!"

Sometimes a man has to put his manly foot down.

So while Michelle wrote toilet-flushing instructions for our houseguest and prepared a small apologetic basket of fruit and cookies, I tried to locate the valve that would shut off all the water. This was very difficult, because our plumbing system turns out to have approximately one valve for every water molecule. We could start a roadside tourist attraction ("TURN HERE FOR THE AMAZING VALVE FOREST").

The fascinating thing is, not one of these valves controls the flow of water to our particular house. I shut a number of them off, and nothing happened. So if, on a recent Sunday, the water stopped flowing in your home or store or nuclear power plant, that was probably my fault.

Since I could not turn off our water, our ceiling continued to leak all Sunday night, so that by morning our bedroom carpet was a federally protected wetland habitat teeming with frogs, turtles, Mafia-hit victims, etc. So we were very happy when the plumber arrived. And if you are a student of literary foreshadowing, you know exactly what he did: He looked at the ceiling, went outside, got a ladder, climbed up on the roof, and found some water sitting up there. It couldn't drain because there was a little place clogged by leaves. The plumber fixed it in maybe 10 seconds. I could have easily fixed it myself at any time in the previous 24 hours if I had not been so busy repairing our plumbing. I wrote the check in a manly manner.

So far Michelle, showing great self-restraint, has said "I told you so" only about 450,000 times. Fine. She's entitled. But don't YOU start on me, OK? Not if you want me to turn your water back on.

The Toilet Police

If you call yourself an American, you need to know about a crucial issue that is now confronting the U.S. Congress (motto: "Remaining Firmly in Office Since 1798"). This is an issue that affects every American, regardless of race or gender or religion or briefs or boxers; this is an issue that is fundamental to the whole entire Cherished American Way of Life.

This issue is toilets.

I'm talking about the toilets now being manufactured for home use. They stink. Literally. You have to flush them two or three times to get the job done. It has become very embarrassing to be a guest at a party in a newer home, because if you need to use the toilet, you then have to lurk in the bathroom for what seems (to you) like several presidential administrations, flushing, checking, waiting, flushing, checking, while the other guests are whispering: "What is (your name) DOING in there? The laundry?"

I know this because I live in a home with three new toilets, and I estimate that I spend 23 percent of my waking hours flushing them. This is going on all over America, and it's causing a serious loss in national productivity that could really hurt us as we try to compete in the global economy against nations such as Japan, where top commode scientists are developing super-efficient, totally automated household models so high-tech that they make the Space Shuttle look like a doorstop.

The weird thing is, the old American toilets flushed just fine. So why did we change? What force would cause an entire nation to do something so stupid? Here's a hint: It's the same force that from time to time gets a bee in its gigantic federal bonnet and decides to spend millions of dollars on some scheme to convert us all to the metric system, or give us all Swine Flu shots, or outlaw tricycles, or whatever. You guessed it! Our government!

What happened was, in 1992, Congress passed the Energy Policy and Conservation Act, which declared that, to save water, all U.S. consumer toilets would henceforth use 1.6 gallons of water per flush. That is WAY less water than was used by the older 3.5-gallon models—the toilets that made this nation great; the toilets that our Founding Fathers fought and died for—which are now prohibited for new installations. The public was not consulted about the toilet change, of course; the public has to go to work, so it never gets consulted about anything going on in Washington.

But it's the public that has been stuck with these new toilets, which are saving water by requiring everybody to flush them enough times to drain Lake Erie on an hourly basis. The new toilets are so bad that there is now—I am not making this up—a black market in 3.5-gallon toilets. People are sneaking them into new homes, despite the fact that the Energy Policy and Conservation Act provides for—I am not making this up, either—a $2,500 fine for procuring and installing an illegal toilet.

I checked this out with my local plumber, who told me that people are always asking him for 3.5-gallon toilets, but he refuses to provide them, because of the law.

The irony is that I live in Miami; you can buy drugs here simply by opening your front door and yelling: "Hey! I need some crack!"

Here's another irony: The federal toilet law is administered by the U.S. Department of Energy. According to a *Washington Post* article sent in by many alert readers, the DOE recently had to close several men's rooms in the Forrestall Building because—I am STILL not making this up—overpressurized air in the plumbing lines was *causing urinals to explode.* That's correct: These people are operating the Urinals of Death, and they're threatening to fine *us* if we procure working toilets.

The public—and this is why I love this nation—is not taking this sitting down. There has been a grass-roots campaign, led by commode activists, to change the toilet law, and a bill that would do that (H.R. 859—The Plumbing Standards Act) has been introduced in Congress by Representative Joe Knollenberg of Michigan. I talked to Representative Knollenberg's press secretary, Frank Maisano, who told me that the public response has been very positive. But the bill has two strikes against it:

1. It makes sense.
2. People want it.

These are huge liabilities in Washington. The toilet bill will probably face lengthy hearings and organized opposition from paid lobbyists; for all we know it will get linked to Whitewater and wind up being investigated by up to four special prosecutors. So it may not be passed in your lifetime. But I urge you to do what you can. Write to your congresshumans, and tell them you support Representative Knollenberg's bill. While you're at it, tell them you'd like to see a constitutional amendment stating that if any federal agency has so much spare time that it's regulating toilets, that agency will immediately be eliminated, and its buildings will be used for some activity that has some measurable public benefit, such as laser tag.

So come on, America! This is your chance to make a difference! Stand up to these morons! Join the movement!

Speaking of which, I have to go flush.

Smuggler's Blues

I say it's time our "leaders" in Washington stopped blathering about sex and started paying attention to the issues that really MATTER to this nation, such as whether we should declare war on Canada.

I say: yes. I base this position on a shocking document that I have obtained via a conduit that I will identify here, for reasons of confidentiality, only as "The U.S. Postal Service." Here is a direct quote from this document:

> STEP ONE: Before inflating Passionate Pam, be sure to smear plenty of . . .

Whoops! Wrong document! I meant to quote from an article in the July 1998 issue of *Contractor* magazine, which was sent to me by alert reader Steve Hill. The article, written by Rob Heselbarth, begins:

> WINDSOR, ONTARIO—Americans are crossing the Canadian border near Detroit to purchase 3.5-gallon-per-flush toilets.

That is correct: Canada has become a major supplier of illegal 3.5-gallon toilets. These toilets were banned by Congress in 1992 under the Energy Policy and Conservation

Act, which decreed that henceforth U.S. citizens had to buy 1.6-gallon toilets, which would conserve a lot of water if they worked, which unfortunately most of them don't, the result being that U.S. citizens now spend more time flushing their toilets than on all other forms of exercise combined.

But that is not the point. The point is that 1.6-gallon toilets are the law of the land, and as the late Supreme Court Justice Felix Frankfurter stated: "Just because Congress passes a stupid law, that is no excuse for awwwggh." Unfortunately, Justice Frankfurter died at that point, but most legal scholars believe he intended to finish his sentence by saying ". . . that is no excuse for people to go up to Canada and buy working toilets."

Yet that is exactly what is happening. The *Contractor* article quotes a Canadian plumbing wholesaler as follows: "We've definitely seen an increase in the sales of 3.5-gallon toilets. The people who buy them are mostly from the States. They tell us outright they're Americans who came here to buy them."

The article quotes officials of both the Department of Energy and the Environmental Protection Agency as stating that it is illegal to bring these toilets into the U.S. But it also quotes a Customs Service official as saying that Customs makes NO EFFORT to confiscate the toilets. "As long as they tell us they have them," the official said, "it makes no difference to us."

In other words, people can simply waltz across our borders with illegal toilets supplied by ruthless Canadian toilet cartels headed by greed-crazed Canadian toilet kingpins who will stop at nothing to push their illicit wares on our vulnerable society. If you are a parent, consider this chilling scenario: Your child is attending a party, when another youngster—a "bad apple"—approaches and says, "Psst! Wanna try a 3.5-gallon

Canadian toilet? All the other kids are doing it!" The next thing you know, your child is acting furtive and sneaking off to a "bad part of town" whenever nature calls. Your child is *hooked*.

Perhaps your parental reaction is: "My little Tommy would NEVER do a thing like that!" Well, let me ask you a couple of questions:

—Do you fully comprehend the power of peer pressure?
—Are you aware that your child is not named "Tommy"?
—Did you realize that "peer pressure" was a toilet-related pun?

If you answered "yes" or "no," then maybe you are beginning to see why we, as a nation, need to send a clear message to the Canadians, in the form of either a sternly worded letter or a nuclear strike. Strong words, you say? Perhaps you will change your mind when you hear what ELSE Canada is exporting. I refer to an article sent in by alert reader Joe Kovanda from the June 1998 issue of *Farm Times*, reporting that Canada's foreign trading partners were complaining that shipments of Canadian feed barley contained excessive amounts of—get ready—deer excrement. The headline for this article, which I am not making up, states:

DEER MANURE IN BARLEY MIFFS JAPANESE

So there is little doubt that the entire world, or at least Japanese barley purchasers, would stand with us if we put a stop to Canada's criminal reign of terror; if we finally stood up to Canada and said:

"Listen, Maple Breath, we are FED UP with your efforts to DESTROY OUR WAY OF LIFE with your LARGE, WORKING TOILETS and your EXCESSIVE DEER DOOTS, which by the way would be an EXCELLENT NAME FOR A ROCK BAND."

Some other advantages of declaring war on Canada are (1) It's one of the few foreign nations that average U.S. citizens—even possibly the CIA—can locate on a map; and (2) Professional ice hockey would be canceled. There's virtually no downside! So I urge you to call your elected representatives TODAY and tell them, in no uncertain terms: "I am strongly in favor, although don't ask me of what." Also let them know that we, the people, don't want to hear another word about this Washington sex scandal. Or, if we HAVE to hear more, how about some new episodes? Speaking of which, I have to go; Passionate Pam has sprung a leak.

Head to Head

As an American, I am feeling pretty darned proud of my country (America). I will tell you why: my new toilet.

I wound up with this toilet as a result of a column I wrote last year, in which I complained bitterly about the new toilets that we Americans had been saddled with as a result of an act of Congress (official motto: "100 Senators; 435 Representatives; No Clues"). This was the Energy Policy and Conservation Act of 1992, which decreed that all new toilets had to use 1.6 gallons of water per flush—less than half the amount of water that the old toilets used. This was supposed to save water.

Unfortunately, the new toilets have a problem. They work fine for one type of bodily function, which, in the interest of decency, I will refer to here only by the euphemistic term "No. 1." But many of the new toilets do a very poor job of handling "acts of Congress," if you get my drift. They often must be flushed two or three times, and even more if it is an unusually large act of Congress, such as might be produced by a congressperson who recently attended a fund-raising dinner sponsored by the Consolidated Bulk Food Manufacturers. The result is that these new toilets were not only annoying, but in some cases seemed to be using MORE water than the old ones.

So I wrote a column complaining about this, and

expressing support for a bill, introduced by Representative Joe Knollenberg of Michigan, that would allow us to go back to toilets that have the kind of flushing power that made America the most respected nation on Earth.

You know how cynics claim that Americans are just a bunch of TV-sedated zombie slugs who don't care about the issues? Well, I wish those cynics had been standing under my mail slot after my toilet column was published, because they would have been crushed like baby spiders under a freight locomotive. I got a huge quantity of letters—some of them far more detailed than I would have liked—from Americans who care *deeply* about the issue of their toilets, and the vast majority of them HATE the new ones.

Granted, I got a few letters supporting the new toilets, but these were mostly from ecology nuts who, because of their organic granola diets, probably don't even NEED toilets, just whisk brooms. There was also a somewhat snippy editorial about my column in *The Washington Post* (motto: "Even Our Weather Forecast Comes From Anonymous Sources"). But the vast majority of the people who responded agreed strongly with me and were ready to revolt over this issue, just as, in 1773, the courageous Boston Tea Party patriots revolted against British tyranny by throwing 1.6-gallon toilets into the harbor.

Then, about five months after my column appeared, I got a letter from Charles Avoles of Contractors 2000, an association of independent plumbing contractors. He said that a New York City company, Varsity Plumbing, in an effort to find a 1.6-gallon toilet that actually works, built a testing laboratory with room for six toilets side by side. Avoles said that Varsity duplicated all the standard toilet tests, but then, in its quest for the ultimate small toilet—the Tara Lipinski of toilets—Varsity "pushed the criteria even further, straining each model to its limits." It must have been exciting: six toilets, pushing the envelope, going head to head! I don't even want to think about it.

Anyway, according to Avoles, Varsity "found one particular 1.6-gallon toilet that actually works," and the company president, Bobby Bellini, made a one-hour presentation on this discovery at the Contractors 2000 annual meeting (as Avoles put it: "Picture 500 people in a hotel ballroom watching videos of toilets flushing"). Contractors 2000 offered to install one of these toilets in my personal home, and I agreed, on the condition that I would pay full price for it, so that I could write a column about it and claim it as an income-tax deduction.

And so in March a Contractors 2000 member, Anthony Fleming, and his wife, Michele, came to my home and installed a new toilet. I cannot speak highly enough of this toilet. It is an inspiring example of American ingenuity and engineering "know-how." It has become like a member of the family; I have affectionately named it "Maurice." The bottom line is this: If there is an act of Congress that Maurice cannot handle in one flush, I have no personal knowledge of it.

I can't use this column for advertising, so I won't specify the brand of the toilet, but you can write to Contractors 2000, 2179 Fourth Street, St. Paul, Minnesota, 55110. By the time you read this, there will probably be other brands of 1.6-gallon toilets that can get the job done; you can ask your plumbing contractor. Of course, by the time you read this, Congress may have passed a new law, requiring that toilets must flush with a maximum of four teaspoons of water, AND be equipped with air bags. Congress is just full of acts.

Gone to the Dogs

Recently it was my great honor to serve as a judge in the Key West Kritter Patrol Dog Show, which is considered one of the most prestigious dog shows held in the entire Key West area on that particular weekend.

This is not one of those dog shows in which serious, highly competitive dog snobs enter professional dogs that can trace their lineage back 153 generations and basically spend their entire lives sitting around being groomed and fed, like Zsa Zsa Gabor. The Key West show—it benefits the Kritter Patrol, a local group that finds people to adopt stray dogs and cats—reflects the relaxed attitude of Key West, where the term "business attire" means "wearing some kind of clothing." This is a show for regular civilian dogs, most of whom, if you had to identify them, technically, by breed, would fall under the category of: "probably some kind of dog."

These are not pampered show animals, but hard-working, highly productive dogs that spend their days industriously carrying out the vital ongoing dog mission of sniffing every object in the world, and then, depending on how it smells, either (a) barking at it; (b) eating it; (c) attempting to mate with it; (d) making weewee on it; or, in the case of small, excitable dogs, (e) all of the above.

When I arrived at the show, the last-minute preparations were proceeding with the smooth efficiency of a soccer riot. There were dozens of dogs on hand, ranging in size from what appeared to be cotton swabs with eyeballs all the way up to Hound of the Baskervilles. Naturally every single one of these dogs, in accordance with the strict rules of dog etiquette, was dragging its owner around by the leash, trying to get a whiff of every other dog's personal region. This process was complicated by the fact that many of the dogs were wearing costumes, so they could compete in the Dog and Owner Look-Alike category. (There are a number of categories in this show, and most of the dogs compete in most of them.) Many owners were also wearing costumes, including one man with an extremely old, totally motionless, sleeping Chihuahua; the man had very elaborately dressed both the dog and himself as (Why not?) butterflies. The man wore a sequined pantsuit, antennae, and a huge pair of wings.

"Look at that!" I said to the other judges, pointing to the butterfly man.

"Oh, that's Frank," several judges answered, as if this explained everything.

Perhaps you are concerned that I, a humor columnist with no formal training or expertise in the field of dogs, was on the judging panel. You will be relieved to know that there were also two professional cartoonists, Mike ("Mother Goose & Grimm") Peters and Jeff ("Shoe") MacNelly, both of whom have drawn many expert cartoons involving dogs. Another judge, named Edith, actually did seem to know a few things about dogs, but I believe she was not totally 100 percent objective, inasmuch as her own dog, Peggy, was entered in most of the events. Edith consistently gave Peggy very high ratings despite the fact that Peggy is—and I say this with great affection and respect—the ugliest dog in world history.

I think she might actually be some kind of highly experimental sheep. Nevertheless, thanks in part to Edith's high marks, Peggy did very well in several categories, and actually *won* the Trick Dog category, even though her trick consisted of—I swear this was the whole trick—trying to kick off her underpants.

Actually, that was a pretty good trick, considering the competition. The majority of the dogs entered in the Trick Dog event did not actually perform a trick per se. Generally, the owner would bring the dog up onto the stage and wave a dog biscuit at it, or play a harmonica, or gesture, or babble ("C'mon, Ralph! C'mon boy! Sing! C'mon! Woooee! C'mon! Wooooooeeee! C'mon!") in an increasingly frantic but generally futile effort to get the dog to do whatever trick it was supposed to do, while the dog either looked on with mild interest, or attempted to get off the stage and mate with the next contestant. My personal favorite in the Trick Dog category went to a very small, very excited poodle named Bunny whose trick, as far as I could tell, consisted entirely of jumping up and down and making weewee on a towel.

As you can imagine, it was not easy serving as a judge with so many strong contestants, both on the stage and hiding under the judges' table. Nevertheless, when it was all over, approximately 43 hours after it started, we had to pick one dog as Best in Show. It was a big decision, and although there was a strong and objective push for Peggy, we decided, after agonizing for close to three-tenths of a second, to give the top prize to Sam, the old, totally motionless, sleeping Chihuahua dressed as a butterfly to match his owner, Frank. Frank got quite emotional when he accepted the trophy, and we judges were touched, although we did ask Frank to make Sam move his paw so we could see that he was, in fact, sleeping, and not actually deceased. Because you have to have standards.

The Nose Knows

Of all the human senses—sight, hearing, touch, taste, and the feeling that a huge man with a barbecue fork is lurking in the closet—perhaps the least appreciated, yet most important, is our sense of smell.

How does our sense of smell work? The simplest way to explain it without doing any research is as follows: Every living thing—animals, plants, cheese, magazine advertisements, etc.—is constantly giving off tiny invisible pieces of itself, which scientists call "smell particles." Suppose that you have just entered a room that contains a fudge brownie. As you approach the brownie, your nose snorks up smell particles from it and passes them along into the Olfactory Canal, which was completed in 1825 and goes to Albany, New York.

No, sorry, wrong canal. The Olfactory Canal takes the particles to your brain, which is actually a fabulously complex computer, which means that on January 1, 2000, it will stop working and your body will flop around like a recently caught perch. But until then, your brain is able to detect the presence of the brownie particles, and, after analyzing them via a subtle electrochemical process involving billions of tiny neural circuits performing highly sophisticated, lightning-fast calculations, produce the following thought: "Yum!"

Your brain then transmits a signal to your hand, telling

it to go ahead and put the brownie into your mouth; almost instantaneously, your hand responds with the signal informing your brain that you ate the brownie several minutes earlier, because your hand and your mouth agreed many years ago that, as far as chocolate is concerned, there is no need to involve your brain.

Thus we see that our sense of smell is not as important as it seemed to be back at the start of this article. In fact, our sense of smell can actually be dangerous, because it stands to reason that if our nose inhales too many particles into our brains, eventually a dense particle wad will form inside us, and our heads will explode, sending compressed brownie chunks hurling outward fast enough to pass through a brick wall. Fortunately, according to a recent study by the American Medical Association, the chances that this will ever happen to you are "less than one in four" provided that "you do not breathe too much."

But the question remains: Why do we have a sense of smell in the first place? The answer is that smell once played a vital role in the survival of the human race, back when we were primitive beings who ran around naked. No, I am not talking about the '60s; I am talking about prehistoric times, when primitive men had to hunt for food to feed their families. They'd creep along naked through the underbrush, and every few minutes they would pause to sniff the air for the scent of prey. Of course, since this was nearly a million years before the invention of soap, all they could smell was their own armpits; the animals could easily detect them at a range of 35 miles. As a result, the hunters never captured any animal that had not already died of natural causes, although when the hunters brought this animal back to the primitive village, they'd make up a story to impress the women with their bravery and prowess.

"Whew!" they would say. "You should have seen the ferocious fight this wild animal put up!"

"That wild animal is a rotting squirrel," the women would respond, "and you get it out of this primitive village RIGHT NOW."

Men and women are still divided on the issue of smell. Most women are very sensitive to odors, whereas men, largely as a result of smelling their own selves over the eons, have reached the point where they tend not to detect any aroma below the level of a municipal dump. That's certainly the way it is in my household. At least five times per week, my wife and I have the same conversation. Michelle says: "What's that smell?" And I say, "What smell?" And she looks at me as though I am demented and says: "You can't SMELL that?"

The truth is, there could be a stack of truck tires burning in the living room, and I wouldn't necessarily smell it. Whereas Michelle can detect a lone spoiled grape two houses away. When she takes food out of the refrigerator, she always sniffs it, and she immediately discards it if it smells remotely suspicious. I, on the other hand, will cheerfully eat a cold cut that was manufactured during the Aztec empire.

This Male Smelling Deficiency Syndrome, or MSDS, explains why women generally smell pretty good, whereas some men, particularly men who sit next to you on airplanes, smell like the Football Team Laundry Bag From Hell. Perhaps you know somebody who tends to emit B.O. rays, and you have been wondering what is the best way to tell him. The answer is: sensitively.

For example, in 1964, when I was a student at Pleasantville High School, I had a class with a teacher who had a major odor problem, to the point where, when he'd stroll past the rows of desks, which he did often, students would keel over in his wake. Being teenagers, we might have handled this situation in a cruel manner. But instead, one day, as the teacher walked past, a student in the front row, whose name I will not reveal here, sensitively whipped out a can of Right Guard brand deodorant, fired off a brief blast, then quickly hid the can before the teacher turned around. This gesture was so sensitive that many of us thought we would rupture key internal organs from vibrating so hard.

There are many, many more exciting facts I could tell you about the fascinating topic of smell, but unfortunately I have no idea what they are. So I will conclude this discussion with this thought: Keep sniffing! But don't inhale.

Missing in Action

I think I might know where the missile launcher is. I'm referring here to the $1 million missile launcher that our armed forces have apparently misplaced, according to the recent audit of the U.S. government (motto: "We Do Have a Motto, But We Don't Know Where It Is").

You might have missed the news stories about this audit, which didn't get a whole lot of media attention because—as difficult as this is to believe—it had nothing to do with Paula Jones. The background is, back in 1994 Congress decided that there should be a complete audit of the entire federal government. This seemed like a good idea, since the U.S. government—which is the fourth-largest financial entity in the world behind Bill Gates, the Spice Girls, and your electrician—had not been audited for (this is the truth) more than 200 years. The reason Congress did not get around to ordering an audit any sooner is that it has been extremely busy with its primary functions, which are (1) spending money; (2) declaring National Cottage Cheese Appreciation Week, and (3) authorizing the IRS to hammer taxpayers for inadequate record-keeping.

As you can imagine, the federal audit was a huge job. The auditors spent thousands and thousands of hours at the U.S. Government Records Facility, which is a 1,400-

foot-long shoe box containing an estimated 139 billion receipts and what are believed to be George Washington's original teeth. When the auditors were finally finished, they released a report that contained a number of alarming findings, including these:

- —It turns out that both "Lewis" and "Clark" were actually the same person, and he never got farther west than New Jersey.
- —Although according to the U.S. Constitution there are supposed to be nine members of the Supreme Court, a detailed search of the premises, including under all the desks, turned up only five.
- —In one three-month period, the Task Force on Reinventing the Government, headed by Vice President Gore, spent, without any formal authorization or supporting documentation, $141 million on party hats.
- —North Dakota is missing. "We think Canada took it," stated the auditors, "but every time we called up there to ask about it, they just laughed and hung up the phone."

Now I have some good news and some bad news. The good news is, I made up the preceding audit findings. The bad news is, the real audit findings are worse. I am NOT referring to the finding that the government has no idea what happened to billions and billions of dollars. That is totally understandable. When you are sucking in and spewing out money as fast as the federal government, you have to expect that here and there a billion dollars is going to fall between the cracks. I bet if federal employees took just a few minutes out of their work schedules to look around, they'd quickly find a lot of this so-called "lost" money.

FIRST FEDERAL EMPLOYEE: OK, I'll just check behind the cushions of this federal employee's lounge sofa here and . . . Hey, here's some! Looks like a total of, let me see, two . . . three . . . four . . . Wow! It's $17 million!

SECOND FEDERAL EMPLOYEE: So THAT'S what happened to it!

So I'm confident that the money is around somewhere. What has me concerned is the auditors' finding that the federal government has also apparently lost track of some fairly large items, including—and I am not making these missing items up—a $1 million Army missile launcher, two $4 million Navy engines for fighter aircraft, two large Navy tugboats costing $875,000 each, and a $460,000 floating crane.

Now, in any organization you're going to have people stealing pens, paper clips, etc. But security has to be pretty darned lax for somebody to walk off with a *tugboat*.

GUARD: Hey, what's that gigantic bulge under your overcoat with a smokestack sticking out?

THIEF: This? Nothing.

GUARD: OK, then.

What concerns me is, what if we have a defense emergency, and we need these missing items? Are we going to scare Saddam Hussein if our fighter pilots have to sit on the runway in engine-less planes and make fighter-plane noises with their mouths? Also, if the government doesn't know where its crane is, what ELSE doesn't it know? For example, I was in Washington, D.C., recently, and I walked past a huge building that said "Department of the Interior"; then a short while later I walked past ANOTHER huge building that said "Department of the Interior."

This has to be a mistake. Why would we need TWO Departments of the Interior? We only have one Interior! Unless we've lost THAT, too.

So I think the government should stop whatever else it's doing until it finds all this missing property. I think a good place to start looking would be my garage. There's a LOT of stuff in there, and I have no idea what most of it is; it would not surprise me one bit if there was a missile launcher in there somewhere. So I say to the government: Come and get it! And while you're here, please take these Supreme Court justices, because they're starting to smell.

Why Abe Was a Geek

It's back-to-school time, parents, and you know what that means! It's time to get the kids off the TV-room sofa, using logging equipment if necessary, and take them to the mall for back-to-school supplies.

Getting the right school supplies is crucial to your child's chances for success in life. We all remember the tragic story of young Abraham Lincoln, whose family could not afford school supplies, so he had to write on a shovel blade with a piece of coal. This meant that if young Abe saw a cute girl and wanted to pass her a note in class, he had to hand her this big gross filthy digging implement, sometimes with worm parts stuck to it, and she'd go, "Ewwww!" and all the other kids would laugh at Abe (it did not help that he was the only boy in the fifth grade who had a beard). As a result, Abe had low self-esteem and was so desperate for popularity that he became president. Unless you want that kind of thing to happen to your child, you had better get the right kind of back-to-school supplies.

What are the "right kind" of supplies? According to the American Association of School Teachers Who Get The Whole Summer Off and You Don't Ha Ha Ha, to meet federal educational standards, "every item your child takes to school, including dental braces, must be festooned with a licensed cartoon character such as The Little Mermaid or Leonardo DiCaprio."

Your child also needs a backpack or—if you wish to have a truly modern, state-of-the-art schoolchild—an actual airline-style suitcase with a handle and wheels. In my neighborhood I see elementary-school students hauling these things around, and I say to myself, "They're in SECOND grade! What are they CARRYING in there? Fifty-pound Twinkies?" But that is not the point. The point is, American students may not have the best educational test scores when compared to foreign students, or even certain species of foreign plants, but by gosh our kids lead the world in cubic feet of academic carrying capacity.

Also it goes without saying that you cannot send your child back to school without a compass and a protractor. A compass is a thing with a sharp metal point and a little mutant pencil that is always falling out. A protractor is a thing that you always get when you get a compass. It is a centuries-old tradition for children to go back to school with these two devices, even though nobody has the faintest idea what their educational purpose is, other than using the metal point to carve bad words into desks. A spokesperson for the American Compass and Protractor Manufacturers Association told us, "We sell 23 million of these things every September, and we lie awake at night asking ourselves, WHY?"

Another traditional item you should have on your back-to-school list is some kind of notebook. I know there are many kinds of new-fangled "high-tech" notebooks on the market today, but for my money, the old-fashioned three-ring binder that I used as a schoolboy remains, as an educational tool, one of the most useless

things ever invented. I spent basically all of my classroom time from 1955 through 1963 trying to repair
torn notebook paper with those stupid "reinforcing
rings" that were always gumming themselves together
into a little defensive clot. It cannot be coincidence that
during these same years, the Soviet Union surged way
ahead in the Space Race. So whatever you do, do NOT
get your child one of these. Your child would be better
off with a shovel.

Finally, while you're in the school-supplies department, see if they have any of that heavy white paste that
we used in first grade to make art projects. Kids don't
need it for school anymore, but you should pick up a
pound anyway, because it's delicious.

OK! Now that you've got the educational supplies,
it's time to shop for back-to-school clothes. What kinds
of outfits do today's kids want? That's easy! They want
outfits that you really hate. For example, if you have a
daughter, you would prefer for her to go to school
dressed, basically, as a nun; whereas she wants to look
as if she has been rejected for employment by a house of
prostitution on the grounds of looking too slutty. How
do you, as a parent, resolve this dispute? According to
the American Association of Child Psychologists, the
secret is to "discuss your differences with your daughter, openly and non-judgmentally, until the two of you
are screaming at each other and she stomps away shouting at the top of her lungs that she hates you and is
going to join a motorcycle gang." Don't worry about
attracting attention: There will be at least 50 other
sets of parents and daughters in the Junior Department
doing the same thing. It's a back-to-school tradition!

Buying clothes for boys is much easier. What boys
want to wear is—write this down—big pants. A good
rule of thumb is, if the pants do not contain enough

material to make all the sails needed to equip a full-sized 19th-century whaling vessel, then those pants are too small for your modern American boy.

OK! You're all done with your back-to-school shopping! Now it's time to send the kids off to school. Even if school doesn't technically start for several more days, shove the little rascals out the door and lock it. Because you've had a long, noisy summer, and you deserve a chance to just lie quietly on the sofa and relax. Maybe fix yourself a bowl of paste.

Rock of Ages

7/26

I got a call from a guy I know named Carl. It was a cry for help. Carl is a successful man in his 40s, but sometimes even successful people, when they are in need, have to reach out to their friends, and I am proud to consider Carl a friend, even though for my 50th birthday he gave me some kind of reptile egg, which thank God never hatched.

It took some effort for Carl to overcome his masculine pride and tell me what was on his mind. It was something that I believe is on the mind of a lot of guys, although they cannot always admit it.

"I think I want to buy an electric guitar," he said.

At some point or another, almost every guy wants an electric guitar. It would not surprise me to learn that, late at night, in the Vatican, the Pope picks one up and plays "Hang On, Sloopy." Electric guitars exert a strong appeal for guys, because they combine two critical elements:

1. A guitar.
2. Electricity.

Taken separately, these elements have little intrinsic value. But combined, they have an almost magical effect: They enable a mediocre guitar player, or even a bad guitar player, to play WAY louder.

I got seriously into electric guitars in the '60s when, as a college student, I helped start a band called "The Guides," which later became "The Federal Duck," which later became "A Bunch of Guys Who Got Older and Developed Prostate Concerns." We were a "psychedelic" band, which means that we sounded a lot better if you were on drugs, not that I am for one second suggesting that anybody was.

As a member of that band, my artistic dream was essentially the same dream that inspired legendary musicians such as Bach, Beethoven, Mozart, and The Dave Clark Five: The dream of getting a bigger amplifier. This was important because of the musical dynamics of a rock band, which are very similar to the political dynamics of the Asian subcontinent. Let's say that India is the drummer, and Pakistan is the lead guitar player. There is always tension between these two instruments, because they both want to be the loudest. Let's say that, in this band, they start out roughly equal, but then, one day, India goes out and gets larger drumsticks. Pakistan is naturally threatened and responds by buying a more powerful amplifier. Then India, seeking to regain superiority, buys even *larger* drumsticks, and maybe a cowbell. At this point the bass player (China) feels it has no choice but to escalate, and pretty soon the band is so loud that merely by tuning up it can kill whales swimming thousands of miles away. (In a selfless effort to avoid this kind of tragedy, The Federal Duck almost never tuned up.)

My point is that I have a strong musical background, which is why Carl called on me in his hour of need. We met at a warehouse-sized musical superstore containing hundreds of electric guitars, not to mention amplifiers the size of public housing. If you live near one of these stores, you'd better hope there never comes a time when all the amplifiers get cranked up simultaneously, because the resulting crater would measure several miles across.

Carl and I spent a while looking at guitars, with me offering knowledgeable insights such as "Here's a guitar," and "Here's another guitar over here." Then a sales man helped us out, explaining various technical aspects of guitars such as wood type, body style, pickups, tuning pegs, necks, frets, etc. Carl listened carefully, then, after considering all the factors, made his decision.

"I want a red one," he said.

So he got a guitar. It came as part of a complete rockstar set in a cardboard box, which also included a strap, picks, and an amplifier. I was concerned about the amplifier, because it was small and probably not powerful enough to cause permanent ear damage. But we agreed that Carl could get a bigger one if he ever learns how to actually play.

I called Carl a week later to see how he was doing. He told me he'd run into a problem.

"I opened the box," he said, "and the guitar was *blue*."

Despite this setback, he was plugging away. He's learning how to play chords from a videotape instructor. ("He's about 18 years old," says Carl. "He has acne.") Once he's done with the tape, he'll be able to play "House of the Rising Sun." Then he can start a band and play at weddings ("As the bride and groom cut the cake, we'd like to play 'House of the Rising Sun' ") as well as bar mitzvahs ("As you all dance the hora, we'd like to play 'House of the Rising Sun' ").

I think there are a lot of older guys like Carl and me and the Pope, older guys still fantasizing that we're Jimi Hendrix (who had the good sense to die before he was 30). As we get even older, we're going to need specialized equipment; somebody's going to make a killing selling amplifiers that have large, easy-to-read numbers on the knobs, so we can make sure they're turned all the way up. Also, somebody's going to get REALLY rich selling earplugs to nursing homes.

Mr. Language Person on Nitches, Yores, and Defective Sea Lions

It is with great verisimilitude that we present another installation of "Ask Mister Language Person," the column that answers your common questions about grammar, punctuation, and unwanted body hair. This is the ONLY language column to receive the coveted Lifetime Bathroom Pass from The American Society of University Professors Who Are Never in Their Offices.

We will commence the onset of today's column by beginning with our first question, which concerns a basic rule of business grammar:

Q. What is the proper way to begin a formal letter?

A. The proper beginning, or "salutatorian," for a formal business letter is: "Dear Mr. or Ms. Bob Johnson as the Case May Be." This should be followed by a small dab of imported mustard.

Q. What if the person's name is not "Bob Johnson"?

A. Then he or she will just have to change it.

Q. What is the correct way to conclude a formal business letter to a cable-television company?

A. "I Spit on Your Billing Department."

Q. Like millions of Americans, I cannot grasp the extremely subtle difference between the words "your" and "you're."

A. Top grammar scientists are often confused by these two words, which are technically known as "bivalves," or words that appear to be identical and have hinged shells. The best way to tell them apart is to remember that "you're" is a contraction, which is a type of word used during childbirth, as in: "Hang on, Marlene, here comes you're baby!" Whereas "your" is, grammatically, a prosthetic infarction, which means a word that is used to score a debating point in an Internet chat room, as in: "Your a looser, you morron!"

Q. What about "yore"?

A. That refers to "the days of yore," when there was a lot of yore lying around, as a result of pigs. Also in those days, men would augment their personal regions by wearing "codpieces," which were pieces of actual cod.

Q. Yuck.

A. Yore telling us.

Q. What is the correct usage of the word "compunction"?

A. It may be used as a medical term ("a compunction of the left exterior vestibule") or in the name of a rock band ("DeWayne Hurlmont and the Compunctions of Soul").

Q. Speaking of music, does it make you suspicious that "Barry Manilow" and "Busta Rhymes," in addition to sounding EXACTLY alike, have "conveniently" never once appeared on stage together?

A. It is time to end the charade.

Q. While viewing ESPN's September 18 broadcast of the Indiana-Kentucky football game, did you hear an example of language usage so excellent that it caused you to spew beer from your nose?

A. Yes. The color commentator referred to a former coach as "a living legend when he was still alive."

Q. Can you give some other examples of powerful language, sent in by alert readers?

A. Certainly:

- Trudy McDaniel sent in the instructions for putting together an Ikea desk, which state: "It is advisory to be two people during assembly."
- Doug Gordon sent in the instructions for a set of Tama brand drums, containing this warning: "Stay away from the drum set if an earthquake occurs."
- Dave Zarrow reports that he saw a sign making this appealing offer: "I Lost 40 Lbs. in Two Months! Call for Free Samples!"
- Joe Bays sent in a glossy color brochure for the American Standard "Cadet II" model commode, featuring the slogan: "Get more out of your toilet."
- Sandra Bowers sent in a story from *The Akron Beacon Journal* headlined "Police Find Man Dead to Death in Motel."
- Paul Morrill sent in a story from *The Santa Cruz County Sentinel*, concerning a man who was arrested when he attacked some sea lions "because they constantly defected on his boat."
- Jeanne Reed sent in a bulletin from Weatherby Health Care, a physician-placement firm, with this headline: "Born and Raised in the Midwest, This Very Talented Surgeon Is Looking for His Nitch Back Home."

Q. You hate it when a surgeon loses his nitch.

A. Let's hope he didn't leave it inside a patient.

TODAY'S "TIP" FOR FICTION WRITERS: To make your writing more vivid, insert a literary device.

WEAK: "Detective Jake Turmoil slowly opened the door to the killer's room."

STRONG: "Detective Jake Turmoil slowly opened the door to the killer's room and a metaphor sliced off his head."

GOT A QUESTION FOR MISTER LANGUAGE PERSON? He truly does not care.

Caught Between a Czech and a Slovakia

Most Americans are pitifully ignorant of geography. This was clearly demonstrated recently when the Gallup Organization sent its pollsters to Chicago to ask randomly selected residents if they could name at least three of the six major continents. The results were shocking: Most of the pollsters never found Chicago at all; of those who did, all but one fell into the Chicago River.

Unfortunately, this is not an isolated incident of American geographical ignorance. Just last month, the major U.S. airlines, investigating an increase in the number of delayed flights, discovered that many of their pilots cannot read maps and are finding their destination cities by, in the words of an airline spokesperson, "flying real low and following buses."

What is the cause of this disgraceful lack of knowledge? I blame the same institution that is responsible for crime, sex, godlessness, and millions of square miles of badly drawn refrigerator art: our school system. I studied geography in the fifth grade, and I remember that instead of just TELLING us where things were, the teacher insisted that we make relief maps of the United States by mixing flour and water into a paste and smearing it on a shirt cardboard so as to form important geographical features such as the Rocky Mountains, the Great Plains, Disneyland, etc. Evidently I put too much water in my paste, because my United States was a featureless amoeba-like blob, with whole population centers such as New England oozing completely off the cardboard and forming new, uncharted territories on the floor.

As a direct result, I grew up, like most Americans, with a poor grasp of geography. That is why, in a recent column about nude TV weather forecasts in the Czech Republic, I made the following statement, which turns out to be incorrect: "Until 1993, the Czech Republic was connected with Slovakia; together they went by the name 'Hungary.' "

This is simply not true, as was pointed out to me by many informed readers. Some of these people were quite upset, as we see from these quotes from their letters, which I am not making up:

- "Clearly, your knowledge of historical facts is a clear example that the dumbing down of America has succeeded."
- "It is disgusting to find out that you columnists know so little. You probably do not know where Vietnam or Indonesia is located. It is not uncommon that the American children do not even know or care where Mexico is situated. And your adults are not better. Thank God, I received my education in Europe."
- "The column's credibility was tainted by the gaffe."
- "How in the world did this get through the editors?"

In response, let me first state that, in the famous words of Thomas Jefferson, "The buck stops here." If there is a gaffe tainting my column, I take full responsibility for it. It is NOT the fault of the editors; I'm sure they never saw it. Modern newspaper editors don't have time to read the newspaper; they spend their days in lengthy "brainstorming" sessions with other editors wherein they try to decide what to do about the Internet.

Second, Mr. "I-Was-Educated-In-Europe": I do TOO know where Vietnam (or, as it is sometimes called, "Indonesia") is located: It is located overseas. So there! And speaking of locating things: If the people in Europe are SOOOOOO smart, how come so many of them can't seem to locate the deodorant, huh?

But there is no need to become petty or defensive. The simple fact is, I "blew it," and I want to set the record straight now: When the Czech Republic and Slovakia were connected, they were called—this now seems SO obvious, when I look at the names "Czech" and "Slovakia" together—"The Netherlands." (Incidentally, this was the original location of the Leaning Tower of Pisa.)

I pledge that from now on I will strive for geographical accuracy in my columns. You parents can also help to raise our national "Geography IQ": The next time your kids ask if they can watch TV or play a video game or take their insulin, you should say: "No! Not until you name all six major continents!" (Answer: America, Central America, South America, Latin America, Euthanasia, and Shaquille O'Neal).

In closing, I wish to apologize to any readers of Czech descent whom I offended by my error. I also want to thank those who sent nice letters, especially Ed Cerny of Conway, South Carolina, who wrote to tell me that at one time the motto of the official Czech airline was: "OK and Getting Better." This really makes me want to go there. By bus.

Parlez-Vous Français?

This summer, for my vacation, I went to Paris, France. I went there to follow in the footsteps of such great writers as Ernest Hemingway, Henry Miller, and "F." Scott Fitzgerald, all of whom, for the record, are currently dead.

I blame the Parisian drivers. Paris has only one vacant parking space, which is currently under heavy police guard in the Louvre museum. This means that thousands of frustrated motorists have been driving around the city since the reign of King Maurice XVII looking for a space, and the way they relieve their frustrations is by aiming at pedestrians, whom they will follow onto the sidewalk if necessary. Often the only way to escape them is to duck into one of Paris's historic cathedrals, which fortunately are located about every 25 feet (or 83.13 liters).

Nevertheless it's very pleasant to walk around Paris and feel—as so many Americans feel when they're in that incredibly beautiful city—fat. Because the fact is that we Americans look like enormous sneaker-wearing beef cattle compared to the Parisians, who tend to be very slim, with an average body weight of 38 pounds (7.83 meters). It's odd that the French appear to be in such good shape, because the major activity in Paris, aside from trying to run over pedestrians, is sitting around in cafés for days at a time looking French.

Sometimes we Americans try to blend in to the café scene, but the French immediately spot us as impostors, because we cannot pronounce the Secret French Code letter, which is "r." They have learned to say "r" in a certain secret way that sounds as though they are trying to dislodge a live eel from their esophagus. It is virtually impossible for a non-French person to make this sound; this is how the Parisian café waiters figure out that you are an American, even if you are attempting to pass as French:

WAITER: *Bonjour. Je suspect que vous êtes American.* ("Good day. I suspect that you are American.")

YOU: *Mais je ne portes pas les Nikes!* ("But I am not wearing the sneakers!")

WAITER: *Au quais, monsieur pantalons intelligents, prononcez le mot "Rouen."* ("OK, Mr. Smarty Pants, pronounce the word 'Rouen.' ")

YOU: *Woon.* ("Woon.")

WAITER: *Si vous êtes français, je suis l'Homme de la Batte.* ("If you are French, I am Batman.")

The other surefire way to tell the difference between French people and Americans in a café is that the French are all smoking, whereas the Americans are all trying to figure out how much to tip. The tourist guidebooks are vague about tipping: They tell you that a service charge is USUALLY included in your bill, but it is not ALWAYS included, and even if it IS included, it is not necessarily TO-TALLY included. On top of that, to convert from French money to American, you have to divide by six, and I have yet to meet anybody who can do this.

And so while the French are lounging and smoking and writing novels, we Americans spend our café time darting nervous glances at the bill, which is often just a piece of paper with a lone, mysterious, not-divisible-by-six number scrawled on it such as "83." We almost always end up overtipping, because we're afraid that otherwise the waiter will make us say another "r" word. I frankly don't know how the French handle tipping, because in my two weeks in Paris I never saw a French person actually leave a café.

Not that I am being critical. As a professional journalist, I like the idea of a society where it is considered an acceptable occupation to basically sit around and drink. In fact, I liked almost everything about Paris. The city is gorgeous, the food is wonderful, and they have these really swoopy high-tech public pay toilets on the streets that look as though, if you went into one, you might get beamed up to the Mother Ship. Also Paris has a terrific subway system, Le Metro (literally, "The Metro"). I always felt safe and comfortable in the Metro, although one time, when I was waiting for a train, the loudspeaker made an announcement in French, which was repeated in English, and I swear this was the whole thing: "Ladies and gentlemen, your attention please. Robbers are in the station. Thank you." None of the Parisians seemed the least bit alarmed, and nobody robbed me, which was a good thing, because I would have had no idea how much to tip.

I have run out of space here, but in next week's column I will tell you about some of the famous tourist attractions of Paris, such as the L'Arc D. Triomphe, Notre Dame, the Leaning Tower of Pisa, etc. So until next week, as the French say, *"Au revoir."* (Literally, "Woon.")

An Aesthetically Challenged American in Paris (Part II)

Today I'll be concluding my two-part series on Paris, France. In writing this series, my goal, as a journalist, is to provide you with enough information about this beautiful and culturally important city so that I can claim my summer vacation trip there as a tax deduction.

My topic in Part II is the historic tourist attractions of Paris. The Parisians have been building historic attractions for more than 1,500 years as part of a coordinated effort to kill whatever tourists manage to escape the drivers. The key is stairs. Most tourist attractions, such as L'Arc de Triomphe (literally, "The Lark of Triumph") and the Hunchback of Notre Dame Cathedral, have some kind of lookout point at the top that you, the tourist, are encouraged to climb to via a dark and scary medieval stone staircase containing at least 5,789 steps and the skeletons of previous tourists (you can tell which skeletons are American, because they're wearing sneakers). If you make it to the top, you are rewarded with a sweeping panoramic view of dark spots before your eyes caused by lack of oxygen. Meanwhile, down at street level, the Parisians are smoking cigarettes and remarking, in French, "Some of them are still alive! We must build more medieval steps!"

Of course the tallest monument in Paris is the Eiffel Tower, named for the visionary engineer who designed it, Fred Tower. The good news is, there are elevators to the top. The bad news is, pretty much the entire tourist population of Europe is up there taking flash pictures of itself. There are so many people crowded into the small-ish observation area that you get the feeling, crazy as it seems, that the whole darned Eiffel Tower is going to topple over. Ha ha! In fact this has happened only twice since 1991.

Paris also has many excellent art museums, the most famous being the Louvre (pronounced "Woon"). If you plan to visit it, you should allow yourself plenty of time to see everything—say, four years—because the Louvre is the size of Connecticut, only with more stairs. The museum contains 30,000 pieces of painting and sculpture, and as you walk past these incredible works of art, depicting humanity through the centuries, you cannot help but be struck, as millions of people have been struck before you, by the fact that for a whole lot of those centuries, humanity was stark naked. To judge from the Louvre, until about 1900, everybody on Earth—men, women, children, gods, goddesses, horses—basically just stood around all the time without a stitch of clothing on. There's one gigantic painting of a bunch of warriors get-ting ready to go into battle, and all they're wearing is swords. You expect to see a comics-style speech balloon coming out of the lead warrior's mouth, saying, "Fight hard, men! If we win the war, we can afford pants!"

I think the reason why the *Mona Lisa* is so famous is that she's just about the only artistic subject in the Lou-vre who's wearing clothes. On any given day, every tourist in Europe who is not on top of the Eiffel Tower is gathered in front of the *Mona Lisa,* who gazes out at the crowd with the enigmatic expression of a person who is pondering the timeless question: "How come they keep taking flash photographs, even though the signs specifically prohibit this?"

I enjoyed the art museums, but for me the most moving cultural experience I had in Paris was—and you may call me a big fat stupid low-rent American pig if you wish—visiting a gourmet food store called Fauchon (pronounced "Woon"), which contains two-thirds of the world's calorie supply. In the great art museums, I eventually reached a saturation point and found myself walking right past brilliant masterpiece paintings by van Gogh, Renoir, Matisse, LeRoy Neiman, etc., without even glancing at them; whereas after a lengthy period of browsing in Fauchon, I was still enthusiastically remarking, with genuine artistic appreciation: "Whoa! Check out THESE éclairs!"

In conclusion, I would say that Paris is the most beautiful city in the world, and its inhabitants have an amazing sense of *"savoir-faire,"* which means, literally, "knowing how to extinguish a fire." I say this because one Sunday afternoon I was in a crowded café when smoke started billowing from a cabinet into which waiters had been stuffing trash. It was a semi-scary situation; I stood up and gestured toward the smoke in an alarmed American manner, but the French diners paid no attention. In a moment, a waiter appeared carrying some food; he noted the smoke, served the food, went away, then returned to douse the fire with, I swear, a bottle of mineral water. And you just know it was the correct *kind* of mineral water for that kind of fire. So the meal ended up being very pleasant. It was also—I state this for the benefit of the Internal Revenue Service—quite expensive.

A Blatant Case of Slanted Journalism

The time has come for us, as a nation, to resolve this wrenching issue, so that we can move on. This issue has been with us for far too long, weighing on our minds, sitting heavy on our hearts, bloating the intestines of our national consciousness with the twin gases of partisanship and hate.

I am referring, as you have no doubt gathered, to the bitter controversy concerning the location of the Leaning Tower of Pisa. This controversy got started last summer when I wrote a column in which I stated that the Leaning Tower of Pisa is located in Paris, France. I received several dozen letters from readers, many of them quite angry, stating that the Leaning Tower of Pisa is in fact located in an Italian city called "Pisa."

Now, I happen to be known in journalism circles as a big stickler for accuracy. I have a stickle the size of a fire hydrant. So when I got these critical letters, I felt that I had no choice but to swallow my pride and send these readers individual notes informing them that they were mistaken, because the Leaning Tower of Pisa had been moved to Paris in 1994. At that point, I assumed that the matter was settled. But then I got *another* letter from one of my original critics, Mrs. Herbert H. Harder of Benton, Kansas. Mrs. Harder's letter, which I am not making up, stated:

"I still don't believe the real original Leaning Tower of Pisa was or ever will be moved to Paris. First of all, I think Pisa, Italy, would never, never allow such a thing to happen . . . To move the Pisa, Italy, real Tower of Pisa would require a cost that would be prohibitive."

To clinch her argument, Mrs. Harder cited the ultimate authority:

"I stopped at a Travel Agency and asked if they had heard anything about the Leaning Tower of Pisa having been moved. Of course, they hadn't."

When you have been in journalism as long as I have (6,000 years), you get used to members of the public making all kinds of wacky claims, such as that the CIA has placed radio receivers in their teeth, or aliens have invaded Earth, or the Leaning Tower of Pisa is located in Italy. So I was frankly inclined to simply ignore Mrs. Harder's letter. But then I got to thinking about a recent public survey about journalism credibility, conducted by the American Society of Newspaper Editors (motto: "Proudly Maintaining the [Motto Continued on Page A-34]"). The ASNE did the survey to find out why the public does not trust us in the news media. The survey showed that you, the public, think that we:

1. Is guilty of many grammar and spelling errores.
2. Rely on what one highly placed ASNE executive described as "too many unnamed sources."
3. Use any excuse to print sensationalistic trash, such as the rumor that reportedly might be printed in an upcoming issue of *Hustler* magazine concerning an allegation that Kenneth Starr got at least 60 percent of the current Spice Girls pregnant.

4. Allow our news judgment to be affected by big advertisers such as General Motors, whose cars are not only fun and reliable, but also prevent cancer.
7. Are just generally careless and sloppy.

The survey also showed that the public thinks these problems have worsened in recent years. I can explain this. In the old days, newspaper stories were checked by editors before being printed; today, editors are busy doing surveys on declining journalism credibility, so they have no time to look at the actual newspaper. (For example, if the phrase "stickle the size of a fire hydrant" appeared in this column, no editor has read it.)

The point is that we have big problems in the news business. But we also have a proud tradition of righting wrongs, expressed in the old saying: "When you make a mistake, have the courage to print a correction that is too small to locate without an electron microscope."

And that is why, when I received the letter from Mrs. Herbert H. Harder of Benton, Kansas, claiming that the Leaning Tower of Pisa is located in Italy, rather than simply tearing it into tiny pieces and feeding them to a hamster, I said to myself, "What if maybe—just maybe—Mrs. Herbert H. Harder of Benton, Kansas, is correct?" And so, after some "nosing around," I uncovered the following information:

- The Leaning Tower of Pisa is, in fact, located in Italy. However, under the Treaty of Ghent, which was signed by Charles "D" Gaulle and Henry VI, Italy is, legally, part of Paris, France.
- The "Leaning" Tower of Pisa is in fact perfectly vertical. All the OTHER buildings in Pisa are leaning, and the residents walk around on special shoes with one heel way higher than the other.

- According to a very highly placed source, both Charles "D" Gaulle and Henry VI got Spice Girls pregnant.

I hope this clears everything up. If you have any questions about this, or any other article in today's newspaper, please do not hesitate to check with your travel agent. Or, if you prefer, you can contact us here at the newspaper directly, via the receivers in our teeth.

Prison Is Deductible

It's time for my annual tax-advice column, which always draws an enthusiastic response from grateful readers.

"Dear Dave," goes a typical letter. "Last year, following your advice, I was able to receive a large tax refund simply by claiming a $43,000 business deduction for 'paste.' I am currently chained to a wall in federal prison, but they tell me that, with good behavior, in 25 years they'll remove the skull screws. Thanks a lot!"

Yes, helping people is what this column is all about.

That's why today I'm going to start by answering a question that taxpayers are constantly asking, namely: "When writing a letter to the IRS, should I use hyphens?"

Not if you can help it. I base this advice on a *Washington Post* news item, sent in by alert reader Bob Pack, concerning an internal memo distributed by the IRS counsel's finance and management division. This memo, according to the *Post,* stated that the deputy chief counsel, Marlene Gross, "does not want to receive any memorandums, letters, etc. with hyphenated words." This was followed by a *second* memo, which stated that Gross "does not want hyphenated words in letters, memos, unless it is at the end of the sentence."

The *Post* item does not say why the deputy chief counsel feels so strongly about hyphens. But it's quite common for people to develop hostility toward certain punctuation marks. I myself fly into a homicidal rage when I see business names featuring apostrophes on either side of the letter "n," such as "The Chew 'n' Swallow Café." Many historians believe the 1970 U.S. invasion of Cambodia was a direct result of the fact that Richard Nixon received a memo containing a semicolon. The important thing for you, the taxpayer, to remember is that if you write a letter to the IRS finance and management division, and you MUST use a hyphen, you should place it at the end of the sentence, as shown in these two example sentences provided by the American Association of Tax Accountants Wearing Suits:

WRONG: "You fat-heads will never catch me!"
RIGHT: "You'll never catch me, fat-heads!"

Speaking of finance and management, I have here an Associated Press story, sent in by many alert readers, concerning a congressional audit of the IRS. The key finding, according to the story, was that the IRS "cannot properly keep track of the $1.4 trillion it collects each year." Isn't that ironic, taxpayers? The IRS—the very same agency that expects you to maintain detailed records of everything but your toenail clippings—can't keep track of $1.4 trillion! Although I'm sure there's a good reason for this. They probably have their hands full at the IRS, what with this hyphen crisis.

But enough about punctuation. Let's answer some other common taxpayer questions, using the popular Q-and-A format.

Q. Are you saying that, as a taxpayer, I *don't* have to maintain detailed records of my toenail clippings?

A. Not if they account for 4.7 percent or less of your Adjusted Gross Bodily Debris, which you are of course required to report quarterly on Form 2038-YUK (not available) unless you are a single taxpayer filing jointly or vice versa, whichever comes first.

Q. Are we EVER going to have a federal tax system that regular people can understand?

A. Our top political leaders have all voiced strong support for this idea.

Q. So you're saying it will never happen?

A. Right.

Q. At 9 A.M. today, I made large cash contributions to both major political parties. As of 1:30 this afternoon, the federal government had still not enacted special tax-break legislation just for me. What kind of country is this?

A. Unfortunately, because of the high demand, the federal government can no longer provide "same-day service," but if you do not see action by noon tomorrow, you should contact your personal congressperson;

or, if you are staying in the Lincoln Bedroom, simply stomp on the floor.

Q. I have been trying without success since 1962 to get through on the IRS Taxpayer Assistance Hot Line. I understand that the IRS now also has a help site on the Internet.

A. That is correct. Now, in addition to failing to receive help by phone, taxpayers can fail to receive additional help by trying unsuccessfully to connect with the IRS World Wide Web site at http://www.bunch-ofletters.gov.

Q. If I *could* get through to that Web site, what would I see?

A. Photographs of Senator Orrin Hatch (R-Utah) naked.

Q. When you write columns like this, don't you worry that the IRS is going to get ticked off and audit you with an electron microscope?

A. No, because the guys and gals at the IRS are a fun bunch, and they know I'm just kidding around. "Ha-ha," is their reaction, unless they work in the finance and management division, where their reaction, if they know what's good for them, is "Ha ha."

How to Handle the IRS

It is time once again for our annual feature "Tax Advice for Humans," the column that explains our complex federal tax laws to you in simple, everyday terms that have virtually nothing to do with reality. This is the only tax-advice column that has the courage to give you the following written guarantee in writing:

"If, as a result of following the advice in this column, you are for any reason whatsoever confined to a federal prison, we will personally come and live in your house, until your refrigerator is out of beer."

So let's get started! Most likely the foremost question in your mind, as you prepare to fill out your federal tax forms, is: "Can I cheat?" A lot of taxpayers are thinking that this is a good year to take advantage of the Internal Revenue Service, because of the way it got hammered in those congressional hearings last September. Remember? One by one, taxpayers went before the Senate Finance Committee and told alarming stories like this:

"I got a letter from the IRS computer stating that I owed taxes back to the year 427 B.C., which seemed like a mistake, plus the letter addressed me as 'The Dionne Quintuplets,' so I went down to the IRS office to straighten things out, and the next thing I knew I was being dangled from a helicopter by one leg."

When the nation heard these stories, everybody was outraged. The IRS formally apologized to the taxpayers and ordered the dismantling of the agency's primary guillotine.

So a lot of people are thinking that this year, while the IRS is under fire, is a good time to "play fast and loose" with their tax returns, and maybe even get revenge for the years of abuse by yanking the IRS's chain a little bit. One leading tax-preparation firm, which I will not identify here except by its initials, "H" and "R," has gone so far as to write taunting remarks in the margins of its clients' tax returns, such as:

— "Hey Audit Breath! If you don't believe I spent a 100 percent deductible total of $224,123 on Pez, perhaps you would like me to complain to the Senate Finance Committee?"
— "No I shall NOT enclose Form 10448275-J! I shall use Form 10448275-J for INTIMATE HYGIENE PURPOSES HAHAHAHA!"

This kind of thing is of course a lot of fun, but we are not recommending it. What many people do not realize is that, after the IRS finished publicly apologizing to the taxpayers who testified against it last September, it quietly tracked them down and relieved them of all of their worldly possessions including corneas.

So we are not recommending that you cheat. You should heed the words of IRS commissioner Charles Rossotti, who, in this year's Letter to Taxpayers, states: "Every citizen owes it to the nation to pay his or her fair share of taxes, unless of course he or she has made a whopping cash contribution to a key congressperson or President Bill 'Mr. Coffee' Clinton or Vice President Al 'I

Honestly Thought That They Were Just A Bunch Of Very Wealthy Buddhist Nuns!' Gore."

Here are some questions that you are likely to ask in preparing your tax returns this year: .

Q. Did the government change the tax laws again?

A. Ha ha! That is the stupidest question we have ever heard! Of COURSE the government changed the tax laws! The government had no choice! The government found out that, despite the fact that the U.S. Tax Code is larger than the entire state of Connecticut, there was still one U.S. taxpayer, Norbridge K. Trongle Jr., who was able to correctly prepare his own tax return. The government considered handling this threat to the national security by sending a B-2 "Stealth" bomber to destroy Mr. Trongle's house and financial records, but the Air Force vetoed this plan because of the risk that the $2 billion plane would be brought down by Mr. Trongle's lawn sprinkler. So the House and Senate Joint Tax Mutation Committee swung into action and made a number of significant changes to the Tax Code, which you need to know about.

Q. What, specifically, are these changes?

A. Nobody knows.

Q. How many taxpayers will have their total income-tax payments, for the entire year, used to provide food, housing, transportation, medical care, Secret Service protection, and chew toys for Buddy, the new White House dog?

A. White House spokeshuman Mike McCurry says that the "best estimate" is currently "around 300 taxpayers," but notes that this number could rise significantly "if Buddy is implicated in this Whitewater thing."

Q. In your opinion, what is the single most common error that I am likely to make, as a taxpayer?

A. In our opinion, that would be having "light" beer in your refrigerator.

Coffee, Tea, or Dried
Wood Chips?

I was getting ready to board an early American Airlines flight out of Miami, and they announced that it was going to be "bistro service."

"Please pick up your 'bistro' meal from the cart as you board the plane," they told us.

I honestly wasn't sure what "bistro" meant, but it sounded French, which I thought was a good sign. French food is pretty tasty, except for the snails, which I do not believe the French actually eat. I believe the French sit around their restaurants pretending to eat out of empty snail shells and making French sounds of enjoyment such as "Yumme!" (literally, "Yum!"). But when foreign tourists order this "delicacy," the waiters bring them shells that still contain actual unretouched snails, which the tourists eat, causing the French people to duck under their tables and laugh until red wine spurts from their nostrils.

But other than that, French food is pretty good. So I had high hopes when, on my way to the plane, I stopped at the cart and picked up a paper sack containing my "bistro" meal. I was hungry, because I had not eaten breakfast, because I had arrived at the airport one hour early so that, in accordance with airline procedures, I could stand around.

When the plane took off, I opened my "bistro" sack.

Here are the items it contained: (1) a container of yogurt, (2) a "breakfast bar" made from compressed dried wood chips, and (3) the greenest, coldest, hardest banana I have ever touched in my life. If I'd had a mallet, I could have pounded it straight into a vampire's heart.

So I didn't eat the banana. Needless to say I also didn't eat the yogurt. My guess is, nobody *ever* eats the yogurt: at the end of the flight, the airline people just collect all the unused yogurts and put them back into "bistro" sacks for the next flight. There are containers of airline yogurt still in circulation that originally crossed the Atlantic with Charles Lindbergh.

I did eat the "breakfast bar," because if you're hungry enough, you will eat wood chips. (That's why beavers do it. There is no way they would gnaw on trees if they ever found out about pizza delivery.)

Anyway, the flight was scheduled to go directly to Houston, so finally, after navigating around the sky for several hours, we landed in: New Orleans. The pilot said there was fog in Houston. No doubt it was manufactured by the Fog Generator, which every modern airport maintains right next to the Banana Freezer.

They didn't let the passengers off the plane in New Orleans, possibly for fear that we would run away. So we just sat there for an hour or so, rustling our "bistro meal" sacks and listening to our stomachs grumble. Here's how bad it got: A woman across the aisle from me finally broke down and *ate her yogurt*. I bet this really messed up the accounting when the airline food personnel got ready to re-sack the yogurt for the next flight ("Hey! There's one missing!").

Anyway, we finally took off again and landed in Houston, where we dropped to our knees and gratefully licked crumbs off the terminal floor. So the story ended happily, except for the nagging question that remained stuck in my mind: Why did the airline call it "bistro service"? When I got home, I looked up "bistro." According to my dictionary, it's a French word meaning "a small wine shop or restaurant where wine is served." The image it conjures up is of a cozy little place on a picturesque little street in Paris, with candle-lit tables for two occupied by lovers kissing, drinking wine, enjoying French food, and laughing at snail-eating tourists. Somehow, the airline decided to use this word, of all the words in the world, to describe what was served on my flight.

Why? The answer is: marketing. At some point, American Airlines went to its Marketing Department and said, "We're going to stop serving real food to people, and we need a good name for it." Marketing people love this kind of challenge. Their motto is: "When life hands you lemons, lie." And so they held a brainstorming session, probably at a nice French restaurant, and finally, after a lot of wine, they came up with "bistro service," which sounds a LOT better, from a marketing standpoint, than "a sack of inedible objects."

Giving things ridiculous names is a key marketing tactic. That's why the gambling industry, when it became concerned that people might think it had something to do with gambling, changed its name to the "gaming" industry, as if people go to Las Vegas to play Capture the Flag.

But I think "bistro service" is even better. It may be the best marketing concept I have seen since back in the 1970s, when McDonald's, which does not wait on your table, does not cook your food to order, and does not clear your table, came up with the slogan "We Do It All For You."

With this kind of marketing ingenuity, there is no telling how far we can go. Perhaps someday, when we board our airplane, we will each pick up a box of dirt; this will be called "haute cuisine service." We will take the box without complaining because we are consumers, and our motto is "moo."

Betting on the Ponies

As a parent, I believe it is my responsibility to help my son develop the skills he will need to become a responsible and productive member of society. So I took him to the horse races.

Specifically I took him to Gulfstream Park, a very nice track in Hallandale, where you can bet on horses and feel comfortable wearing clothing styles dating back upward of 45 years. You remember during the Disco Age, when men wore clingy pants in highly unnatural colors and patterns, so that the wearer looked as though he has been wading naked to his waist in a massive toxic polyester spill, and it dried on his body? Those pants are still the height of style, at the racetrack. We are talking about an older crowd, including guys who, at some point in their betting careers, bet on a Trifecta involving Spartacus.

I enjoy the racetrack crowd. It's a more sociable group than you might think. I'm generally shy, but when I go to the track, I often find myself having conversations with total strangers. I'll be standing idly near a bank of TV monitors showing horses racing—possibly at this track; possibly at some other track; possibly in races that took place in 1973—and a man standing next to me will suddenly yank his cigar out of his mouth, turn to me, and say: "Can you believe THAT?"

"No!" I'll say.

"What the (bad word) is he DOING??" the man will say. "He's (bad word) CRAZY!!"

"I'll say!" I'll say, wondering whom we're talking about. A horse? A jockey? Newt Gingrich?

"You're (bad word) RIGHT he's (bad word) crazy!" the man will say, glad to have encountered somebody else who knows what's going on. Then he'll walk away, still talking, leaving behind no clues except a small puddle of cigar drool.

I began the process of educating my son, Rob, by showing him how to pick a horse to bet on. The key is to have a system. I use what is known as a "two-step" system, as follows (you might want to write this down):

1. I look at a list of the various horses.
2. I pick one.

Using this system, I selected a horse named "Yield To Maturity," which seemed appropriate because it's something that people are always urging me to do. After I placed the bet, we went into the grandstands to watch the race. Tension mounted as post time drew near, and then the announcement came over the loudspeaker: "They're off!"

"COME ON, YIELD TO MATURITY!" I shouted.

"Where are the horses?" asked Rob.

"I don't know," I had to admit. One of the problems with horse racing is that key parts of the race take place several miles away, so that even if you can find the horses, they look like a herd of stampeding squirrels. I think the sport would be better if the horses stayed directly in front of the grandstand, perhaps on a treadmill.

Eventually the horses showed up, and although I specifically yelled at Yield To Maturity to win, he (or possibly she) did not. What's worse, he (or possibly she) did not look the least bit upset about losing. In fact none of the horses seemed to take the race seriously. Laughing and pooping, they trotted gaily off the track and headed for the horse locker room to call their brokers. They're all into conservative mutual funds.

Next I took Rob outside to show him how to "look over" the horses that would be running in the next race.

"What are we looking for?" asked Rob.

"Humps," I said. A hump indicates to the shrewd bettor that the horse is actually a camel, which means it will run slower than the horses. Or possibly faster; I can never remember which.

At this point Rob decided—and this is exactly the problem with young people today; they don't want to learn anything—that he was going to ignore my system and pick his own horses by (Get this!) studying the racing form. I told him this was a waste of time, because the so-called "racing form" in fact has nothing to do with racing: It's a means by which espionage agents send each other messages in secret code. Here's an actual quote from the form that Rob was studying:

"Magic Way has the highest Beyer in the field, which is a nice starting point at the maiden level."

Right! And the Presbyterian mollusk wears linen jodhpurs!

While Rob was frittering away his time trying to decipher gibberish, I implemented another proven wagering system, known as the "bet on most of the horses in the race system." Perhaps you think that it is impossible to bet on six horses in an eight-horse race and still not win any money. Perhaps you are an idiot.

I will not beat around the bush. When the day was over, I had picked no winning horses, no placing horses, and no showing horses. I had picked horses that, if you were to cut them open—and don't let me stand in your way—would have turned out to be powered by pairs of seriously obese men walking backward. Rob had picked three winning horses and ended up making money. He thinks this could be a good career path. He does seem to have a knack for it. I just hope, if he becomes wealthy, that he remembers who showed him the ropes.

My Son's College Apartment Has a Pleasant Pepperoni Motif

So I visited my son at college on Parents Weekend, which is a nice event that colleges hold so that parents will have a chance to feel old.

I started feeling old the moment I got to my son's housing unit and saw a sign on the door that said: END WORLD HUNGER TODAY. This reminded me that there was a time in my life, decades ago, when I was so full of energy that I was going to not only END WORLD HUNGER, but also STOP WAR and ELIMINATE RACISM. Whereas today my life goals, to judge from the notes I leave myself, tend to be along the lines of BUY DETERGENT.

I felt even older when I entered my son's apartment, which he shares with three roommates and approximately 200 used pizza boxes. When I was a college student, we also accumulated used pizza boxes, but we threw them away after a reasonable period of time (six weeks). Whereas my son and his roommates apparently plan to keep theirs forever. Maybe they believe that a wealthy used-box collector will come to the door and say, "If you can produce a box used to deliver pizza on the night of September 12, 1999, I'll pay you thousands of dollars for it!" Because they WILL have that box on file.

They keep their pizza boxes in the kitchenette, which is also where they keep their food supply, which is an open jar containing a wad of peanut butter as hard as a bowling ball. You may be wondering: "What happens if a burglar breaks into the kitchenette and steals their pizza boxes?" Do not worry. They keep a reserve supply of pizza boxes in the living room, and if a burglar tried to get *those*, he'd trip over the cord that stretches across the room from the TV to the video-game controller held by a young man who is permanently installed on the sofa. This young man is not one of my son's roommates; for all I know, he's not even a student. But he is stationed in the living room 24 hours a day, focused on the video game, although he always gives you a polite "Hi" when you walk through the room and step over his cord. I'm not familiar with the game he's playing, but I noticed, as I stepped over the cord, that the screen said: "YOU HAVE BEEN AWARDED EIGHT THUNDERS." Maybe this has something to do with world hunger.

After passing through the living room, I stuck my head into my son's bedroom. I was reluctant to enter, because then I'd have been walking on my son's clothes. He keeps them on the floor, right next to the bureau. (I don't know what he keeps in the bureau. My guess is: pizza boxes.) My son assured me that, even though his garments appear to be one big intertwined pile, he knows which are clean and which are dirty.

"Like, this one is clean," he said, picking a garment off the floor, "and this one is clean, and this one is . . . never mind."

There were no sheets on my son's bed. Asked about this, he explained (this was the entire explanation): "They came off a couple of weeks ago."

I'm not complaining about my son's housekeeping. He is Martha Stewart compared with the student who occupied his bedroom last year. According to true campus legend, when this student moved out, his laundry was so far beyond human control that he simply abandoned it. As a kind of tribute, his roommates took a pair of his briefs outside, climbed a lamppost, and stretched the briefs over the lamp. They remain there today, a monument to the courage and dedication it takes to put underpants on a lamppost. I was gazing up at them in admiration when a student said to me: "That's the cleanest they've ever been."

Not all student rooms look like my son's. Some are occupied by females. If you stand outside the building, you notice that those rooms have curtains and pictures on the walls; whereas the males' rooms have all been painstakingly decorated with: nothing. The only designer touches are lines of bottles, and the occasional tendril of laundry peeking coyly over a windowsill. We stood outside my son's building one evening, noting this difference; my son, looking at a tasteful, female-occupied room, said, with genuine wonder in his voice: "I think they vacuum and stuff."

Speaking of which: During Parents Weekend, I took my son shopping, and we bought, among other things, a small vacuum cleaner. When we got back to his room, one of his roommates opened the box and held up the vacuum cleaner. We all looked at it, and then at the room. Then we enjoyed a hearty laugh. Then the roommate set the vacuum cleaner down on the floor, where it will be swallowed by laundry and never seen again. This is fine. These kids are not in college to do housework: They are there to learn. Because they are our Hope for the Future. And that future is going to smell like socks.

The Gulf Between Father and Son Is Called "Quantum Physics"

Recently I received a phone call from my son, Rob. It was a phone call that every parent dreads.

That's right: My son told me that the universe does not exist. Or at least it does not in any way resemble my concept of it. According to Rob, I understand the universe about as well as a barnacle understands a nuclear aircraft carrier.

I blame college. That's where Rob is getting these ideas, which have to do with the Theory of Relativity and something called "quantum physics." Rob and his roommate, Hal, stay up all night discussing Deep Questions and figuring out the universe, and when they have it nailed down—The Rob and Hal Theory of Everything—Rob calls me up, all excited, and starts talking about time travel, the Fifth Dimension, the Big Bang, etc. I try to follow him, but I am hampered by a brain that for decades has firmly believed that the Fifth Dimension is the musical group that sang "Up, Up and Away." So I quickly become confused and testy, and Rob gets frustrated and says, "Don't you understand? THERE'S NO SUCH THING AS TIME!" And I'll say, "YES THERE IS, AND RIGHT NOW IT'S FIVE O'CLOCK IN THE MORNING!"

(At one point—I swear this is true—we got into a

bitter argument about whether people in Minneapolis age at the same rate as people in Miami.)

When I was in college, during the '60s, there was no such thing as "quantum physics." Or, if there was, nobody told ME about it. Back then, when we stayed up all night, we were not trying to figure out the universe: We were trying to figure out how to operate the phone, so we could order pizza. (Note to young people: Phones were MUCH more complicated in the '60s.)

I was an English major, and when we English majors thought about physics, we were trying to solve problems like: "You are required to turn in a 15-page paper on *The Brothers Karamazov*. You have written a grand total of 311 words on this topic. How big do you have to make your margins to make these words stretch over 15 pages? Do you think the professor will notice that your 'paper' is a little anorexic worm of type running between margins wide enough to land an airplane on? Do you think that anybody in history has ever actually read all the way to the end of *The Brothers Karamazov*? Why?"

This is not to say that I know nothing about physics. I studied physics for an ENTIRE YEAR in Pleasantville High School under the legendary Mr. Heideman. We learned that there are five simple machines: the lever, the pulley, the doorbell, the hammer, and the toaster. We learned that the most powerful force in the universe is static electricity, which Mr. Heideman demonstrated by getting a volunteer to place his or her hand on a generator, which caused the volunteer's hair to stand on end, unless the volunteer was a girl with the popular early '60s "beehive" hairstyle held rigidly in place by the other most powerful force in the universe, hair spray. Presumably, if Mr. Heideman had cranked the power up enough, the static electricity buildup would have caused the volunteer's head to explode, and we would finally have found out if—as widely rumored—many "beehive" hairstyles contained nests of baby spiders.

Thanks to my high-school training, I believed I had a solid grasp of physics. So when Rob was growing up, I was able to answer his questions about the universe, such as "What is a star?" (Answer: a big ball of static electricity that has caught on fire because of friction with comets) or "What is gravity?" (Answer: a powerful type of static electricity that sucks you toward the ground, especially after you eat Italian food).

These answers satisfied my son until he started reaching that snotty, know-it-all age when kids start losing all respect for authority (18 months). And now he's calling me from college and telling me that the universe is NOTHING like my concept of it. The stuff he talks about is pretty complex, but I will try to summarize the main points, as I understand them:

- Point One: Whatever you think about anything is wrong.
- Point Two: There is no such thing as Point One. You THINK there is a Point One, but that just shows what a physics moron you are.
- Point Three: If there are identical twins, and one of them gets on a spacecraft going at nearly the speed of light, then one of them will grow old much faster than the other, and that one will retire to Miami.
- Point Three: There is an infinite number of possible Point Threes, and they are all equally true, and you will never understand ANY of them.

OK? Is that clear to everybody? Good! To prove you really understand, I want you all to write me a 15-page paper on how the universe works and send it backward through time to me in 1964, c/o Mr. Heideman's class. OK, I got it. Thanks.

"Day Trading For Dummies," Including Nap Times, Bankruptcy Laws

How would you like to make BIG MONEY while sitting at home in your bathrobe eating cake frosting straight from the can whenever you felt like it?

If this sounds like the ideal career to you, then you should get into "online trading," which means getting rich by buying and selling stocks on the Internet, a world-wide network of computers operated by magic.

I assume you are on the Internet. If you are not, then pardon my French, but *vous êtes un big loser*. Today EVERYBODY is on the Internet, including the primitive Mud People of the Amazon rain forest. In the old days, when the Mud People needed food, they had to manually throw spears at wild boars; whereas today they simply get on the Internet, go to www.spear-a-boar.com and click their mouse a few times (the Mud People use actual mice). Within three business days, a large box is delivered to them by a UPS driver, whom they eat.

So you, too, need to get online, and it could not be easier! Signing up with an Internet Service Provider (ISP) takes only a few minutes, after which you will immediately start enjoying all the benefits of having a fee charged to your credit card every month until the end of time. If you wish to cancel your account for any reason, such as your death, all you have to do is contact your ISP, fill out a simple form, then climb into a big tank and fight Rex, the Customer Service Death Squid.

But you won't have to worry about monthly fees once you're making "big money" as an online trader! Of course financial experts recommend that, before you make any investment decision, you should carefully read a "Q&A"-type column written by a trained English major. Here it is:

Q. Are there any risks associated with online stock trading?

A. Yes. People do get hurt. To cite just one example: A man whom I will call Webster P. Horngasket II of 2038 Open Wound Lane, Eau Claire, Wisconsin, who was unemployed and had a wife and five hungry children to support, took his last $17.40, which was supposed to be for little Jessica's insulin, and decided to "play the market" with it, despite having no previous experience. Two days later, his lifeless body was found crushed under an enormous pile of thousand-dollar bills that he had failed to stack properly.

Q. What a chilling cautionary tale.

A. His family had to go to Disney World without him.

Q. How should I choose an online brokerage?

A. You'll be trusting your brokerage with your financial future, so you should make absolutely sure that you pick one with a good TV commercial.

Q. What about the brokerage whose commercial for some reason consists entirely of people square-dancing?

A. That is an excellent firm, although every now and then the staff has to run out and assist in the birth of a heifer.

Q. OK, I've chosen an online brokerage! Now what do I do?

A. Step one in your investment program, according to the American Society of Financial Planners, is to quit your job. "The best way," notes the Society, "is to write a businesslike letter of resignation and staple it firmly to your immediate supervisor's forehead." Now you're ready to get rich by trading stocks!

Q. What, exactly, ARE stocks?

A. They are pieces of paper stating that you, personally, own a piece of a company. This means that if you own stock in, say, General Motors, any time you want, you may walk into a Chevrolet dealership and take a piece of a car.

Q. What if I own stock in NBC?

A. You may touch Jennifer Aniston's thighs.

Q. What is the best strategy for buying stocks?

A. Consider the story of two neighbors, "Bob" and "Ted," who each have $5,000 to invest. "Bob" invests in a diversified portfolio of solid stocks with prospects for steady long-term growth; while "Ted" gambles it all on a single high-risk stock. After six months, during which the Dow Jones Industrial Average has risen by 14.3 percent, "Bob" falls to his death while attempting to unclog his gutters, and "Ted" suddenly realizes that he does not have to return "Bob's" riding mower.

Q. So it's better to just let the gutters stay clogged?

A. That has always been our philosophy.

Q. What causes the Stock Market to go up and down?

A. A man named Alan Greenspan. If he's in a good mood, the market goes up; if he's in a bad mood, the market goes down.

Q. So you're saying I should put uppers in his Metamucil?

A. That is how Martha Stewart did it.

Q. Can you give me the name of a "sleeper" stock that you know, from "inside" information, is about to go through the roof?

A. Yes, and here it is, unless the newspaper editors decide to keep it to themselves.

Stay Tuned to FearPlex, for More Panic All Day, Every Day

NEWS ANNOUNCER: Good evening. Our top story tonight is Tropical Depression Vinny, which is shaping up to be the most deadly potential natural disaster ever to strike this nation since last week when Tropical Depression Ursula came within just 1,745 miles of American soil before veering off and inflicting an estimated $143 worth of damage on the Azores. For more on Vinny, let's go straight to the FearPlex WeatherCenter, where meteorologist Dirk Doppler, in anticipation of a long night of escalating tension, has already applied 75 cubic feet of Rave Extra Hold hair spray.

METEOROLOGIST: Thank you, Bill. As we can see from this satellite photograph taken from space, right now Vinny is located at a latitude of 36.8 degrees centigrade and is projected to follow a path that, according to our computer model, could potentially take it directly to any of the 13 original colonies as well as Florida, Kentucky, Oklahoma, Canada, and western Europe. We are urging everybody within the potentially affected area to become extremely nervous, because this thing potentially has the potential to become a Category Seven storm, which means a storm capable of yanking the udder right off a standing cow.

ANNOUNCER: What is your best guess at this point, Dirk?

METEOROLOGIST: Without creating undue alarm, Bill, I would say there is no hope for human survival on this planet.

ANNOUNCER: Thank you, Dirk. We go now to reporter Crystal Baroque, who has been standing by at the Homeowner Hell megastore. Crystal?

REPORTER: Bill, as usual with storms of this potential, there are long lines of people waiting to buy plywood. Sir, how long have you been here?

CUSTOMER: I've been waiting 17 hours, but it's worth it, to get plywood. Whenever there's a storm, I hear these voices telling me, "Irving! Go get plywood!" And I don't even have a home! I just have a big pile of plywood.

REPORTER: I see.

CUSTOMER: Also, my name isn't "Irving."

REPORTER: Back to you, Bill.

ANNOUNCER: In another important tradition, the supermarkets are jammed with panicked consumers buying bottled water, as you see in this videotape that we have shown during every potential storm since 1973. Now let's go back to the FearPlex WeatherCenter for an update from meteorologist Dirk Doppler.

METEOROLOGIST: Bill, as you can see from this satellite photograph, Tropical Depression Vinny has not moved at all, which means we are now expanding the potential disaster area to include mainland China. The satellite is also reporting the entire planet Earth is surrounded by a cold, airless void extending for trillions of miles in all directions. It looks very bad, Bill.

ANNOUNCER: We now go to the National Hurricane Center, where we'll be speaking with the director,

Harmon Wankel, who has been sitting in the same chair for 68 straight hours without food or sleep, staring into bright lights while being relentlessly interviewed by TV news people about this potential storm. Harmon, what's the latest word?

HURRICANE CENTER DIRECTOR: I hope you all die.

ANNOUNCER: Thank you. Now we're going to go to the White House, where we understand President Clinton is about to make an emergency statement.

THE PRESIDENT: As you can tell by my big, sad moony face, my heart goes out to all of those who have the potential of being devastated by this potentially devastating storm. I have ordered the mandatory evacuation of North and South America, to be enforced by strafing, and I have personally instructed Vice President Gore to get into a helicopter and fly around until everybody in his entourage is airsick. I am also hereby offering clemency to every convicted felon in New York State. Let us all bite our lips and pray that this terrible potential disaster proceeds directly to the home of Kenneth Starr.

ANNOUNCER: Let's go back to the FearPlex Weather-Center, where Dirk Doppler has an Urgent News Bulletin on Tropical Depression Vinny.

METEOROLOGIST: Bill, according to our latest satellite images, Vinny is gone! It was right here, and now, pffft, there's no sign of it!

ANNOUNCER: Does this mean we can stop panicking?

METEOROLOGIST: Of course not. Vinny could be *anywhere*. It could be *in your house*. Everybody should get under the bed NOW. Also we need to start worrying about potentially lethal Tropical Breeze Xera, which is forming over here. See it?

ANNOUNCER: No.

METEOROLOGIST: YES YOU DO! IT'S RIGHT THERE! YOU'VE GOT TO BELIEVE ME!

ANNOUNCER: We go now to Dan Rather, courageously standing on a beach, wearing a slicker.

The Wait for the Tub Is Forever
Since the Frogs Moved In

I'm wondering if any of you readers out there have noticed any suspicious behavior on the part of frogs. I ask because the ones at my house are definitely up to something.

I live in South Florida, which has a hot, moist, armpit-like climate that is very favorable for life in general. Everything down here is either already alive, or about to be. You could leave your toaster out on your lawn overnight, and by morning it would have developed legs, a tail, a mouth, tentacles, etc., and it would be prowling around looking for slower, weaker appliances to prey on.

So I am used to wildlife. I am used to the fact that, as I walk from my car to the front door—striding briskly to prevent fungus from growing on my body—I will routinely pass lizards, snakes, spiders, snails, and mutant prehistoric grasshoppers large enough for the Lone Ranger to saddle up and ride into the sunset on ("Hi-yo, Silver, AWAYYYEEEIIKES!").

My yard has also always had plenty of frogs. Until recently, these were plump, nonaggressive frogs who just sat there, looking pensively off into the distance, thinking frog thoughts. ("How am I supposed to reproduce? I appear to lack organs!")

But lately my yard has become infested with a whole new brand of frogs—smaller, quicker, junior-welterweight frogs that are extremely jittery, as though they spent their tadpole phase swimming around in really strong espresso. And for some reason these frogs desperately want to *get inside my house*. They hide in crannies on my front stoop, waiting, and when I open the front door, suddenly HOP HOP HOP HOP HOP, the stoop turns into the Oklahoma Land Rush, except that instead of hardy pioneers racing to claim homesteads, there are hordes of small, caffeine-crazed frogs bounding into my living room, moving far too fast for the human foot to stomp on.

The eerie thing is, within seconds, the invading frogs have *all disappeared*. Some go under the sofa, but many seem to simply vanish. I think maybe they've developed some kind of camouflage, so they can blend into the living-room environment by taking on the appearance of a carpet stain or (if they are really organized) a piano.

All I know is, the frogs go into my house, and they do not come out, which means that there are now, by conservative estimate, thousands of frogs hiding somewhere in my living room. This makes me nervous. I'm wondering if maybe it could be a plague.

I say this because my wife is Jewish, and each year her family comes to our house to celebrate Passover with a traditional Seder feast. I am not Jewish, but I always join in, on the theory that you should embrace as many religions as possible, because you never know. You could die and find yourself in an afterlife facing the eternal judgment of, for example, L. Ron Hubbard. So I participate in the Seder; in fact, at our house I always make the traditional matzoh balls, using an ancient Presbyterian recipe. (The matzoh balls symbolize the Old Testament story about how the Israelites, after following Moses all over the desert, finally came to a place where there was chicken soup.)

Anyway, there's this one point in the Seder ceremony when we all dip our fingers into our glasses of ancient, traditional Manischewitz wine, and then we drop 10 wine droplets onto our plates while we say, out loud, the names of the Ten Plagues of Egypt, which are: blood, darkness, blight, slaying of the firstborn, wild beasts, lice, boils, locusts, hail, and—you guessed it—Leonardo DiCaprio.

No, seriously, one of the plagues is frogs. So I'm thinking that maybe, during the most recent Seder, when we were saying the plague names, we failed to make adequate wine droplets for the frogs. My concern is that this might have violated some clause in the Old Testament, such as the Book of Effusions, Chapter Four, Verse Seven, Line Six, which states: "And yea thou shalt BE sureth to maketh a GOOD frog droplet, for if thou shalt NOT, forsooth thou SHALT getteth a BIG plague of frogs, and they SHALT be of the JUNIOR-welterweight division, and they WILL hideth UNDER thine sofa."

Or maybe there's some other cause. Maybe it's a Y2K issue, and these are noncompliant frogs. Whatever it is, I don't like it. I don't like sitting in my living room at night, watching the TV, knowing that all around me, hidden in the dark, thousands of beady little eyes are also watching the TV . . . and maybe waiting for some secret signal. Perhaps you think I am crazy. Fine. Then perhaps you can explain to me why, when the frogs croak in the Budweiser commercial, my piano croaks back.

A Titanic Splash (Again)

I finally finished the script for the sequel to the movie *Titanic*. I am calling it—and let the legal record show that I thought of this first—*Titanic II: The Sequel*.

I am darned proud of this script. I have been working on it, without sleeping or eating, except for two grilled-cheese sandwiches, for the better part of the last 35 minutes. I realize that sounds like a lot of work, but bear in mind that writer/director James Cameron spent nearly twice that long on the script for the original movie, which was entitled *Titanic I, the Original Movie*.

As you know, *Titanic I* garnered a record 56 Academy Awards, including Best Major Motion Picture Lasting Longer Than Both O.J. Trials Combined; Most Total Water; Most Realistic Scene of Bodies Falling Off The End of a Sinking Ship and Landing on Big Ship Parts With a Dull Clonking Sound; and Most Academy Awards Garnered. The movie has made a huge star out of Leonardo DiCaprio, who has shown the world that he is not just a pretty face; he is a pretty face who, if he had been in my high school, would have spent a lot of time being held upside down over the toilet by larger boys.

The phenomenal success of *Titanic I* has also served as an elegant rebuttal to the critics of writer/director Cameron, although this has not prevented him from going around Hollywood physically hitting these critics on the head with his Oscar statuette. Cameron was especially angry at *Los Angeles Times* film critic Kenneth Turan, who said Cameron's writing was trite and devoid of subtlety; this prompted Cameron to take out a full-page newspaper ad saying, quote, "Bite me."

I certainly don't want to take sides in this issue, other than to say that James Cameron is easily the most talented human being in world history including Michelangelo and Shakespeare and all four Beatles combined. I say this out of a sincere desire to have Mr. Cameron pay a hefty sum for my script for *Titanic II: The Sequel*. Here it is:

(The movie opens with the Titanic II, *getting ready to sail. As the ship's horn blasts a mighty departure toot, up runs spunky young Jack Dawson, played by Leonardo DiCaprio. There is seaweed on him.)*

JACK: Whew! I just made it!

ROSE: Jack! I thought you had drowned! To death!

JACK: No! Fortunately, the bitter North Atlantic cold was unable to penetrate my protective layer of hair gel! Who are you?

ROSE: I'm Rose! Remember? You gave your life for me in *Titanic I.*

JACK: But Rose was played by Kate Winslet!

ROSE: She didn't want to be in another movie with you, because your cheekbones are so much higher! So the part went to me, Demi Moore!

JACK: Whatever.

(The scene shifts to the ship's bridge.)

CAPTAIN: Ahoy First Mate! Commence starboard computer animation! Full speed ahead!

FIRST MATE: Sir! We're getting reports of gigantic icebergs directly ahead! Shouldn't we go slow?

CAPTAIN: Don't be silly! What are the chances that we're going to hit *another* . . .

(There is a loud crunching sound. Big pieces of ice come through the window, along with several penguins.)

CAPTAIN: Dang!

FIRST MATE: Sir! The computerized sinking animation has commenced!

(The scene shifts to the Poop Deck, where the water is rising fast. Jack and Rose are helping women and children into a lifeboat, when an evil villain appears with a gun.)

VILLAIN: Out of the way! I'm taking this lifeboat all for myself!

JACK: It's Kenneth Turan, film critic for the *Los Angeles Times*!

TURAN: That's right, and I shall stop at nothing to get off this ship, because the dialogue is terrible!

JACK: Is not!

TURAN: Is too!

(They commence fighting.)

THE LATE BURGESS MEREDITH: You can do it, Rock! Watch out for the jab!

JACK: Hey! You're in the wrong sequel!

MEREDITH: Sorry!

(This distraction enables Turan, by cheating, to gain the upper hand.)

TURAN: I have gained the upper hand! Whatever that expression means! And now, pretty boy, I'm going to . . . OHMIGOD! NOOO!

(Turan is torn into raisin-sized pieces by an irate horde of young female Leonardo DiCaprio fans.)

JACK: Whew! That was close! Uh-oh! The ship is almost done sinking!

ROSE: This is it! I hope I don't end up as an old bag in this movie!

(As the two lovers start to slip beneath the icy cold computerized waves, they embrace. There is a cracking sound.)

JACK: You broke my ribs!

ROSE: Sorry! I have tremendous upper-body strength since starring in *G.I. Jane*!

JACK: Don't worry! As long as my cheekbones are OK!

(The water slowly closes over them. In the distance, we hear two crew members on a lifeboat, looking for survivors.)

FIRST CREW MEMBER: What's that sound coming from over there?

SECOND CREW MEMBER: It sounds like . . . Oh my God! It's Celine Dion!

FIRST CREW MEMBER: Let's get out of here!

(THE END)

Blair Witch Mystery Solved: The Seal Did It

Recently it came to my attention that I was one of the eight remaining Americans who had not seen *The Blair Witch Project*.

In case you're one of the other seven, I should explain that *The Blair Witch Project* is a hugely popular movie that was featured simultaneously on the covers of both *Time* and *Newsweek* (mottoes: "We Both Have the Same Motto"). *The Blair Witch Project* stunned the Hollywood establishment, because it proved that, to make a hit movie, you don't need big stars, an expensive production, and a huge promotional budget to generate hype. All you need is a huge promotional budget to generate hype. The movie itself can cost $34.

Not wishing to be a cultural holdout, I went to see *The Blair Witch Project*, which tells the story of three young film students who attempt to make a documentary without a tripod. This means the camera constantly moves around, as though it is strapped to the head of a hyperactive seal. (For some reason, the camera is often pointed more or less at the ground, as though the seal is hunting for ants.) The effect of this technique is to create a mood of intense realism for several minutes, after which it creates a mood of intense motion sickness.

The three movie characters are looking for the Blair Witch, who according to legend is a mean witch who is never actually seen because of the high cost of special effects. The characters set out and almost immediately become lost in the legendarily huge uninhabited forests of Maryland (motto: "The Endless Vast Expanse of Wilderness State"). They respond to this predicament exactly as Lewis and Clark would have: by holding long whiny arguments wherein they wave the camera around and repeatedly shout a very bad word that I cannot put in the newspaper, so let's just call it "darn." Much of the dialogue sounds like this:

FIRST CHARACTER: Darn you! You darned got us darned lost in these darned woods! Darn!
SECOND CHARACTER: Go darn yourself!
SQUIRREL: Will you darners shut the darn UP!?!

The characters are all so busy arguing and yelling "Darn!" at each other that, in the entire movie, they actually travel a grand total of maybe 75 linear feet. You get the impression that if they'd just shut up and *walk*, in 20 minutes they'd come to a Wal-Mart. But they don't, and after several days they run out of food. They do NOT, however, run out of electricity for their cameras, which apparently are powered by tiny, highly portable nuclear generators.

And thus they are able to keep videotaping, which enables you, the viewer, to experience the terrifying things that happen right outside their tent at night, namely: It's hard to say. Apparently SOMETHING terrifying is happening, but you can't really tell what it is, because pretty much all you see is the ground, or total darkness. Much of the footage near the end appears to be shot deep inside a sleeping bag.

I won't reveal the terrifying and shocking surprise ending of the movie, because I don't want to spoil it, plus I have no idea what it is, since it's not actually IN the movie. The characters all get killed and are unable to videotape it. But at least the darned camera stopped moving.

I hope I don't appear to be criticizing *The Blair Witch Project*. I happen to think it's a great film, because despite its flaws, it meets the ultimate artistic test: It will make over a hundred million dollars. This inspires me. In my college days, I spent my summers working at Camp Sharparoon as a counselor for disadvantaged youths, and one of my key counseling techniques was terror. When we were out in the woods at night, I could make the youths at least briefly stop hitting each other and making bodily sounds by telling them scary bedtime stories. Not to brag, but some of my stories were a lot scarier than *The Blair Witch Project*, as determined by the standard unit of measurement for bedtime-story scariness, which is Bedrolls Wetted.

So I'm thinking I can cash in on my Camp Sharparoon stories by turning them into terrifying low-budget films. I'll start with *Hunt for the Latrine Demon*, which will be about an ill-fated attempt to make a documentary about an entity that dwells, according to legend, in a primitive hand-dug campsite toilet facility. I've already got a script written ("It's got me by my darned ankles!"). All I need now is some unknown actors, a video camera, and a huge promotional budget. And of course a seal.

A Rolling Stone

So get this: I partied with Mick Jagger. Well, OK, perhaps "partied with" is too strong a term. Perhaps a better term would be "was in the vicinity of." But still. Mick Jagger!

The way this happened was, back in December I got a fax from a public-relations agency inviting me to a party being given by a person named Chris Blackwell, who is very famous although I honestly still don't know why. The fax said that the purpose of the party was to celebrate the "new incarnation" of the Marlin Hotel, which is a swank night spot in an area of Miami Beach called South Beach, a chic, avant-garde jet-set sector where you never see a woman who is under six feet three or weighs more than 83 pounds. This is a place where Barbie would look like a middle linebacker.

The invitation said: "Among the guests expected are The Rolling Stones, as they're in town for their concert this Friday."

Of course I wanted to go to this party. I have been a gigantic Rolling Stones fan since approximately the Spanish-American War. In college, I was in a rock band called The Federal Duck, and we performed many Stones songs, and at the risk of tooting my own horn, I will say that we sounded exactly the way the Stones themselves would have sounded if they were not all playing the same chords.

On the night of the party, my wife was out of town, so I asked my 17-year-old son, Rob, if he wanted to go with me. You can imagine his excitement when I offered him a chance to meet the Rolling Stones IN PERSON.

"No thanks," he said.

Like many young people of today, my son does not appreciate classical musicians such as the Stones; he is more into bands with names like "Heave" and "Squatting Turnips." So I asked a friend, novelist Paul Levine, if he wanted to go to the party, and he courageously said yes, despite the very real risk that I would, in this column, mention his forthcoming book 9 *Scorpions*, which Paul describes as "a story of seduction and corruption at the Supreme Court." (I just hope that this description does not cause anybody to envision William Rehnquist naked.)

Paul and I arrived at the Marlin Hotel and immediately determined that we were the oldest people who had ever set foot in there by a good 30 years. The party featured very loud music and many avant-garde people lounging around amid the new, reincarnated hotel decor, which included, among other sophisticated touches, window treatments that looked like gigantic shower curtains. We did not see any Rolling Stones. But there were several famous people on hand, including:

—An artist named Kenny something whose work "is in like museums all over the place."
—An actor named Antonio something who had been in a Janet Jackson video AND a Calvin Klein underwear commercial.

Paul and I got this information from a 20-year-old woman hair stylist named Nate (pronounced "Na-TAY"), who also gave us both free advice on what to do with our hair. She told Paul to use gel. She told me—and this is a direct quote—"You should rock the Caesar."

"I should rock the Caesar?" I asked.

"Definitely," said Nate.

"You really should," said Paul.

It turns out that "rock the Caesar" means getting the style of haircut worn by the Roman emperor Julius Caesar and the TV actor George Clooney. I definitely plan to adopt this style, just as soon as William Rehnquist does.

So anyway, Paul and I were sitting in a corner, a pair of fossils with outmoded hair, when the front door opened, and guess who walked in, in all his rock-idol glory? That's right: Elvis.

No, seriously, it was Mick Jagger. When I saw him, I felt a thrill, and I will tell you why: Because suddenly, there was somebody at the party who was even older than I am. He's only a little older if you calculate it in normal human years; but he has been living rock-star years, which take a much greater toll. In person, he looks like Yoda wearing a Mick Jagger wig.

But he seemed like a pleasant enough person, as near as I could tell from watching a crowd of avant-garde people trying to get as close to him as possible while pretending not to. I considered trying to push my way in there and strike up a conversation with Mick, maybe try to find out the correct chords to "Under My Thumb." But it seemed like a lot of work, plus it was 10:30 P.M., way past my bedtime. So Paul and I left. But I enjoyed the evening. The way I see it, I was, briefly, hanging out with an actual Rolling Stone. If you see it differently, get offa my cloud.

Decaf Poopacino

I have exciting news for anybody who would like to pay a lot of money for coffee that has passed all the way through an animal's digestive tract.

And you just know there are plenty of people who would. Specialty coffees are very popular these days, attracting millions of consumers, every single one of whom is standing in line ahead of me whenever I go to the coffee place at the airport to grab a quick cup on my way to catch a plane. These consumers are always ordering mutant beverages with names like "mocha-almond-honey-vinaigrette lattespressacino," beverages that must be made one at a time via a lengthy and complex process involving approximately one coffee bean, three quarts of dairy products, and what appears to be a small nuclear reactor.

Meanwhile, back in the line, there is growing impatience among those of us who just want a plain old cup of coffee so that our brains will start working and we can remember what our full names are and why we are catching an airplane. We want to strike the lattespressacino people with our carry-on baggage and scream "GET OUT OF OUR WAY, YOU TREND GEEKS, AND LET US HAVE OUR COFFEE!" But of course we couldn't do anything that active until we've had our coffee.

It is inhumane, in my opinion, to force people who

have a genuine medical need for coffee to wait in line behind people who apparently view it as some kind of recreational activity. I bet this kind of thing does not happen to heroin addicts. I bet that when serious heroin addicts go to purchase their heroin, they do not tolerate waiting in line while some dilettante in front of them orders a hazelnut smack-a-cino with cinnamon sprinkles.

The reason some of us need coffee is that it contains caffeine, which makes us alert. Of course it is very important to remember that caffeine is a drug, and, like any drug, it is a lot of fun.

No! Wait! What I meant to say is: Like any drug, caffeine can have serious side effects if we ingest too much. This fact was first noticed in ancient Egypt when a group of workers, who were supposed to be making a birdbath, began drinking Egyptian coffee, which is very strong, and wound up constructing the pyramids.

I myself developed the coffee habit in my early 20s, when, as a "cub" reporter for the *Daily Local News* in West Chester, Pennsylvania, I had to stay awake while writing phenomenally boring stories about municipal government. I got my coffee from a vending machine that also sold hot chocolate and chicken-noodle soup; all three liquids squirted out of a single tube, and they tasted pretty much the same. But I came to need that coffee, and even today I can do nothing useful before I've had several cups. (I can't do anything useful afterward, either; that's why I'm a columnist.)

But here's my point: This specialty-coffee craze has gone too far. I say this in light of a letter I got recently from alert reader Bo Bishop. He sent me an invitation he received from a local company to a "private tasting of the highly prized Luwak coffee," which "at $300 a pound . . . is one of the most expensive drinks in the world." The invitation states that this coffee is named for the luwak, a "member of the weasel family" that lives on the Island of Java and eats coffee berries; as the berries pass through the luwak, a "natural fermentation" takes place, and the berry seeds—the coffee beans—come out of the luwak intact. The beans are then gathered, washed, roasted, and sold to coffee connoisseurs.

The invitation states: "We wish to pass along this once in a lifetime opportunity to taste such a rarity."

Or, as Bo Bishop put it: "They're selling processed weasel doodoo for $300 a pound."

I first thought this was a clever hoax designed to ridicule the coffee craze. Tragically, it is not. There really is a Luwak coffee. I know because I bought some from a specialty-coffee company in Atlanta. I paid $37.50 for two ounces of beans. I was expecting the beans to look exotic, considering where they'd been, but they looked like regular coffee beans. In fact, for a moment I was afraid that they were just regular beans, and that I was being ripped off.

Then I thought: What kind of world is this when you worry that people might be ripping you off by selling you coffee that was NOT pooped out by a weasel?

So anyway, I ground the beans up and brewed the coffee and drank some. You know how sometimes, when you're really skeptical about something, but then you finally try it, you discover that it's really good, way better than you would have thought possible? This is not the case with Luwak coffee. Luwak coffee, in my opinion, tastes like somebody washed a dead cat in it.

But I predict it's going to be popular anyway, because it's expensive. One of these days, the people in front of me at the airport coffee place are going to be ordering decaf poopacino. I'm thinking of switching to heroin.

Good for What Ails You

Recently I was lying on the sofa and watching my favorite TV show, which is called, *Whatever Is On TV When I'm Lying on the Sofa*. I was in a good mood until the commercial came on. It showed an old man (and when I say "old man," I mean "a man who is maybe eight years older than I am") helping his grandson learn to ride a bicycle.

I was watching this, wondering what product was being advertised (Bicycles? Dietary fiber? Lucent?) and the announcer said: "Aren't there enough reasons in *your* life to talk to your doctor about Zocor?"

The announcer did not say what "Zocor" is. It *sounds* like the evil ruler of the Planet Wombax. I figure it's a medical drug, although I have no idea what it does. And so, instead of enjoying my favorite TV show, I was lying there wondering if I should be talking to my doctor about Zocor. My doctor is named Curt, and the only time I go to his office is when I am experiencing a clear-cut medical symptom, such as an arrow sticking out of my head. So mainly I see Curt when I happen to sit near him at a sporting event, and he's voicing medical opinions such as "HE STINKS!" and "CAN YOU BELIEVE HOW BAD THIS GUY STINKS??" This would not be a good time to ask him what he thinks about Zocor ("IT STINKS!").

Television has become infested with commercials for drugs that we're supposed to ask our doctors about. Usually the announcer says something scary like, "If you're one of the 337 million people who suffer from parabolical distabulation of the frenulum, ask your doctor about Varvacron. Do it now. Don't wait until you develop boils the size of fondue pots."

At that point, you're thinking, "Gosh, I better get some Varvacron!"

Then the announcer tells you the side effects.

"In some patients," he says, "Varvacron causes stomach discomfort and the growth of an extra hand coming out of the forehead. Also, one patient turned into a lemur. Do not use Varvacron if you are now taking, or have recently shaken hands with anybody who is taking, Fladamol, Lavadil, Fromagil, Havadam, Lexavon, Clamadam, Gungadin, or breath mints. Discontinue use if your eyeballs suddenly get way smaller. Pregnant women should not even be watching this commercial."

So basically, the message of these drug commercials is:

1. You need this drug.
2. This drug might kill you.

I realize that the drug companies, by running these commercials, are trying to make me an informed medical consumer. But I don't WANT to be an informed medical consumer. I liked it better when my only medical responsibility was to stick out my tongue. That was the health-care system I grew up under, which was called "The Dr. Mortimer Cohn Health-Care System," named for my family doctor when I was growing up in Armonk, New York.

Under this system, if you got sick, your mom took you to see Dr. Cohn, and he looked at your throat, then he wrote out a prescription in a Secret Medical Code that neither you nor the CIA could understand. The only person who could understand it was Mr. DiGiacinto, who ran the Armonk Pharmacy, where you went to get some mystery pills and a half-gallon of Sealtest chocolate ice cream, which was a critical element of this health-care system. I would never have dreamed of talking to Dr. Cohn about Zocor or any other topic, because the longer you stayed in his office, the greater the danger that he might suddenly decide to give you a "booster shot."

We did have TV commercials for medical products back then, but these were non-scary, straightforward commercials that the layperson could understand. For example, there was one for a headache remedy—I think it was Anacin—that showed the interior of an actual cartoon of a human head, so you could see the three medical causes of headaches: a hammer, a spring, and a lightning bolt. There was a commercial for Colgate toothpaste with Gardol, which had strong medical benefits, as proven by the fact that when a baseball player threw a ball at the announcer's head, it (the ball) bounced off an Invisible Protective Shield. There was a commercial for a product called "Serutan." I was never sure what it did, but it was definitely effective, because the announcer came right out and stated—bear in mind that the Food and Drug Administration has never disputed this claim—that "Serutan" is "natures" spelled backward.

You, the medical consumer, were not required to ask your doctor about any of these products. You just looked at the commercial and said, "A hammer! No wonder my head aches!" And none of these products had side effects, except Colgate, which, in addition to deflecting baseballs, attracted the opposite sex.

I miss those days, when we weren't constantly being nagged to talk to our doctors, and we also didn't have a clue how many grams of fat were in our Sealtest chocolate ice cream. Life was simpler then, as opposed to now, when watching TV sometimes makes me so nervous that I have to consume a certain medical product. I know it's effective, because it's "reeb" spelled backward.

A Critic, a Crocodile, and a Kubrick—*Voilà!*

As a noted film critic, I assume that you are eager to read my impressions of *Eyes Wide Shut*, the controversial much-discussed final film in the *oeuvre* of Stanley Kubrick, or, as he was known to those of us who considered him a close personal friend before he died, "Stan."

What is one to make of *Eyes Wide Shut*? Is this the *chef d'oeuvre*, the *pièce de résistance* if you will, of this legendary cinematic *auteur*? Does it possess the penultimate exigency, the insouciant *escargot*, the *frisson de voiture* of Stan's earlier work? Or does it succumb to the inevitable *bouillabaisse en route* that every great *roman à clef* experiences when he reaches the point that the great French director Renault Citroën once, in a moment of *pique*, described as *fromage de la parapluie* (literally, "umbrella cheese")?

These are, indeed, some questions. And if one is to truly address them, one has an obligation, as a noted cultural commentator as well as a human being, to have some direct knowledge of the film in question. Thus it was that this critic—reluctantly pausing in his ongoing project of reading the complete unabridged works of Marcel Proust in the original French handwriting in a drafty room with poor lighting—went to the cinematic theater for a personal firsthand viewing of *Eyes Wide Shut*.

This critic will not, as the great Italian director Ronzoni Sono Buoni used to say, "beat around amongst the shrubbery." This critic will come right out—at risk of violating the First Rule of serious cinematic criticism ("Avoid clear sentences")—and tell you exactly what *Eyes Wide Shut* is about: It is about two and a half hours long. That is frankly more time than this critic can afford to spend in a cinema, because at this critic's current rate of cinema-concession-snack consumption (CCSC), which is one box of Goobers per 45 minutes of film viewing, this critic would soon develop what the great German director Audi Porsche Messerschmitt referred to as *ahugengrossenbiggenfattenheinie.* After two and a half hours, it would take a construction crane to hoist this critic back out of his seat.

And so this critic elected to instead view another film playing at the same theater, *Lake Placid,* which is about half as long as *Eyes Wide Shut,* but involves even less actual viewing time if you, like this critic, close your eyes tight for certain scenes, such as the one at the beginning where a scuba diver is swimming in the lake and something grabs him from underwater, so his friend tries to rescue him by pulling him back into the boat, and the only really positive thing you can say about the diver at that point is that, if he had survived, he would never again have had to worry about finding pants in his size, if you get this critic's drift.

Lake Placid explores a classic literary theme—a theme that has fascinated artists from Homer to Shakespeare to Milton to Milton's younger brother, Arnold, namely: What happens when an Asian crocodile swims over from Asia and winds up in a secluded lake in Maine, where it grows to a length of 30 feet?

The answer is: some serious chomping. Because naturally, after the crocodile eats half of the diver in the opening scene, more people immediately show up and insist on swimming in the lake with their legs dangling down invitingly like big fat corn dogs with feet. One of the great mysteries of the cinema is why characters insist on plunging into bodies of water known to contain hungry irate marine life-forms with mouths the size of two-car garages. More than once this critic has been tempted to shout, "GET OUT OF THE WATER, YOU CRETINS!" But of course the characters cannot hear. Also, there was some risk associated with spraying semi-chewed Goobers into the hair of the person sitting in the row ahead.

And so the audience of *Lake Placid*—which, for the showing attended by this critic, consisted mostly of large families who apparently had mistaken the theater for the Playtime Day-Care Center for Loud Hyperactive Children—can only sit and chew helplessly as the crocodile eats various minor characters, not to mention a bear, a moose, and part of a helicopter. This sets the stage for the film's climactic scene, in which—this critic is not making this scene up—the heroes lure the crocodile into a trap by flying the injured helicopter over the lake and dangling from it, in a sling at the end of a long cable, a *live cow*. Not since the heyday of the great Japanese director Nissan Kawasaki has this critic seen a more effective cinematic use of airborne livestock. If that cow does not win an Oscar for Best Supported Actor, then this critic will have some very harsh words for somebody.

In conclusion, *Lake Placid* is a worthy addition to the cinematic *genre* of Movies Where Body Parts Frequently Wash Ashore. As for *Eyes Wide Shut*: Although this critic has not seen it personally, cinematic sources say that it has a certain *je ne sais quoi* (literally, "movie stars naked"). So this critic is giving both of these fine films two thumbs up. That's a total of four thumbs up. So it's a good thing that spares are washing ashore.

Grammar: De Letter of De Law

At this juncture in the time parameter we once again proudly present "Ask Mister Language Person," the No. 1 rated language column in the United States according to a recent J. D. Power and Associates survey of consumers with imaginary steel plates in their heads. The philosophy of this column is simple: If you do not use correct grammar, people will lose respect for you, and they will burn down your house. So let's stop beating around a dead horse and cut right to the mustard with our first question:

Q. I often hear people use the word "irregardless," as in: "Irregardless of what you may or may not think, moths are capable of remorse." So finally I decided to look "irregardless" up in the dictionary, but I can't figure out what letter it begins with.

A. Grammatical experts disagree on this.

Q. What are the correct lyrics to the song "It's Howdy Doody Time!"?

A. According to the Library of Congress, they are as follows:

It's Howdy Doody Time!
It's Howdy Doody Time!

It's Howdy Doody Time!
It's Howdy Doody Time!

Q. Who wrote those lyrics?

A. Cole Porter.

Q. I am in the field of business, and people keep saying they want to "touch base" with me. They'll say, "I just wanted to touch base with you on the Fooberman contract," or "We need to touch base on the rental sheep for the sales conference." But my understanding of the rules is that if you touch base WITH somebody, at the same time, at least one of you is out. So my question is, who the heck is "Fooberman"?

A. We decided to consult with William Safire, one of the top experts in the language field, but his number is not listed.

Q. I am never sure when I should use the word "principle" and when I should use "principal." Is there an easy way to remember the difference?

A. Here's a simple memory device for distinguishing between these two similar-sounding words (or "sonograms"): Simply remember that "principal" ends in the letters "p-a-l," which is an antonym for "Police Athletic League"; whereas "principle" ends in "p-l-e," which are the first three letters in "Please Mister Postman," by the Marvelettes. If this memory device does not work for you, we have a more effective technique involving a soldering iron.

Q. When the Marvelettes sing, *"Deliver de letter, de sooner de better,"* are they using correct grammar?

A. No. The correct grammar would be, *"Deliver de letter, irregardless."*

Q. Did alert reader Johnny G. Stewart send you an

amusing automotive review from the March 12, 1997, Lewiston, Idaho, *Morning Tribune*?

A. Yes. It states: "A short-throw six-speed Borg-Warner transmission means classic Pontiac excitement and the fun of a well-timed shift."

Q. What's so amusing about that?

A. There was a letter missing from "shift."

Q. Can you cite some other examples of language usage sent in by alert readers?

A. Certainly:

—John Triplett sent in a Heartland America catalog advertising baseballs that were "hand-signed by Mickey Mantle before his death."

—W. Michael Frazier sent in an editorial from the December 6, 1997, Huntington, West Virginia, *Herald-Dispatch* containing this statement: "We believe if you have too much to drink at a holiday party, insist on driving yourself home."

—Susan Olp sent in an Associated Press story concerning a lawsuit verdict in which a lawyer is quoted as saying: "It sends a message to gas companies in Wyoming that gas companies better operate safely because people are not going to tolerate being blown up."

—Thomas Caufield sent in an August 11, 1996, *San Jose Mercury News* story about a Stanford University instructor, containing this statement: "Since his suspension, Dolph has continued working as a manager in the university's lab for cadavers. In that position, he deals mainly with faculty members, Jacobs said."

—Several readers sent in a June 19, 1998, Associated Press story concerning a Vermont high-school student who disrobed during her graduation speech; the story quotes school administrators as saying the incident "was not reflective of our student body."

—Renee Harber sent in a police log from the July 24, 1997, Corvallis (Oregon) *Gazette Times* containing this entry: "12:38 P.M. July 20—report that a man near the Crystal Lake boat ramp was threatening to kill the next person he saw wearing a kilt."

TIPS "FOR" WRITERS: In writing a screenplay for a movie, be sure to include plenty of action.

WRONG: "To be, or not to be."
RIGHT: "LOOK OUT! GIANT RADIOACTIVE SQUIRRELS!"

GOT A QUESTION FOR MISTER LANGUAGE PERSON? Send it in, and you could receive a baseball hand-signed by William Shakespeare shortly after his death.

The Unfriendly Skies

For those of you planning to travel by air, here are some amazing statistics about the U.S. airline industry (motto: "We're Hoping to Have a Motto Announcement in About an Hour"). This year, U.S. airlines will carry a record 143 million passengers, who will be in the air for 382 million hours, during which they will be fed an estimated total of four peanuts.

Yes, the airlines are cutting back on food service, as was dramatically demonstrated on a recent New York–to–London flight wherein nine first-class passengers were eaten by raiders from coach. But despite the cutbacks, the U.S. airline industry is still one of the safest on Earth; the only nation with a better safety record is the Republic of Kyrgyzstan, which has only one airplane and can't figure out how to start it.

The U.S. airline industry, in contrast, boasts a vast fleet of modern planes maintained by a corps of highly professional mechanics, by which I mean "mechanics who are all wearing the same color of uniform." This is not the case in some countries. One time I was leaving a Caribbean island aboard a two-propeller airplane owned by an airline with a name like "Air Limbo." As we sat on the runway, getting ready for takeoff, I could not help but notice that an important-looking fluid was gushing out of the engine on my side. This made me nervous, so I was relieved when a man wearing shorts and flip-flops came over to take a look. He studied the fluid, which was really pouring out, then he turned toward the pilot and made the "OK" sign. I was thinking, "OK? WHAT DO YOU MEAN, OK??" And while I was thinking that, *we took off.* We did make it to our destination, but I'm pretty sure we were followed the whole way by a pack of hungry sharks thinking, "That thing can't stay up there much longer!"

You generally don't have to worry about sharks with domestic air travel, but there are things you need to know, which is why today I'm presenting these:

ANSWERS TO COMMON AIR-TRAVEL QUESTIONS

Q. Airline fares are very confusing. How, exactly, does the airline determine the price of my ticket?

A. Many cost factors are involved in flying an airplane from Point A to Point B, including distance, passenger load, whether each pilot will get his own pilot hat or they're going to share, and whether Point B has a runway.

Q. So the airlines use these cost factors to calculate a rational price for my ticket?

A. No. That is determined by Rudy the Fare Chicken, who decides the price of each ticket individually by pecking on a computer keyboard sprinkled with corn. If an airline agent tells you that they're having "computer problems," this means that Rudy is sick, and technicians are trying to activate the backup system, Conrad the Fare Hamster.

Q. When should I arrive at the airport?

A. You should arrive two hours before your scheduled departure time, so that you will be among the first to know that your flight has been delayed due to mechanical problems.

Q. What do they mean by "mechanical problems"?

A. They mean that the pilot cannot find his magic feather.

Q. What precautions will be taken to insure that there is no terrorist bomb aboard my aircraft?

A. The airline agent will ask you a series of security questions shrewdly designed to outwit terrorism, such as: "Did any terrorist unknown to you give you a bomb to carry on board this plane?" Also, if you have a laptop computer, they may ask you to turn it on, thus proving that it is not a terrorist bomb.

Q. But couldn't a terrorist easily put a bomb in a computer in such a way that the computer could still be turned on?

A. Shut up.

Q. What happens to my carry-on baggage when it goes through the X-ray machine?

A. There is a man named Karl crouching inside there who paws rapidly through your belongings.

Q. Looking for terrorist bombs?

A. No. Soiled underwear.

Q. How much carry-on baggage am I allowed to take?

A. In the past, passengers had to be able to physically lift the luggage to carry it on to the plane. But that restriction has been eliminated, thanks to the discovery, by the luggage industry, of wheels. Today, passengers routinely board airplanes towing suitcases the size of sleeper sofas. On a recent TWA flight from St. Louis to Atlanta, a passenger boarded with a Volkswagen Jetta, which he was able to get into the overhead storage bin after just seven hours of shoving.

Q. What is that thumping noise you sometimes hear after takeoff?

A. That is Vomax, Hell Demon of the Cargo Hold. It is nothing to worry about.

Q. Why do they make you bring your seat back to the full upright and locked position?

A. Because they do not like you.

One final thought: Although most of us feel anxiety about flying, it's important to remember that, statistically, commercial airline travel is more than *three times* as safe as snake handling. So buckle up, and have a great flight! I myself will be on Air Kyrgyzstan.

What is El Niño? Will it cause massive climatic changes? Will it ultimately threaten the very survival of humanity? Does it contain fat?

These are just some of the alarming questions that are raised by the phenomenon of El Niño, which in recent months has been blamed for virtually everything abnormal that is happening in the world including the singing group Hanson. To help you understand why you need to become alarmed about El Niño, let's take a moment here to review how the Earth's weather works:

Scientists who study weather—who are called "meteorologists," to distinguish them from scientists who study meteors, who are called "scientists who study meteors"— tell us that weather is caused by the atmosphere, which is a gaseous mixture containing oxygen, nitrogen, monosodium glutamate, and radio waves. Moisture gets into the atmosphere from the oceans by a process called "evaporation," which is caused by whales coming to the surface and blowing their noses, which, because of an evolutionary mistake, are located on top of the whales' heads. In fact, most of a whale's major bodily orifices are located in unusual places, a fact that enables whales to play some hilarious undersea pranks that we cannot discuss in a family newspaper. Suffice it to say that it is considered very funny in whale circles to say "I gave him an earful."

Anyway, after these warm, moist air masses are formed over the ocean, they get pushed eastward by the "jet stream," which is a high-altitude, fast-moving "river of air" constructed in 1958 by the Army Corps of Engineers as part of a federal project intended to prevent commercial airplane flights from being on time. When a warm, moist air mass reaches land, it meets up with a cold, dry, boring air mass from Canada, and these two masses begin a complex ritual in which the male becomes excited and inserts his . . .

No, wait, sorry, that's how salamanders reproduce. What I meant to say is: When an air mass reaches land, it proceeds to a major metropolitan area, where it is struck by radar beams sent out by TV weather forecasters, which cause the evaporated moisture to turn into rain and "sleet," which is actually little frozen pieces of whale snot. So we see that the true cause of bad weather, contrary to what they have been claiming all these years, is TV weather forecasters, who have also single-handedly destroyed the ozone layer via overuse of hair spray.

So where does El Niño come into this picture? We cannot answer that question with total certainty until we have had a couple more beers. But we do know that "El Niño" is a Spanish name, meaning, literally, "The Little Neen." It refers to a seasonal warming of the Pacific Ocean, which is critical to the Earth's fragile ecosystem because it contains more than 80 percent of our dwindling supply of anchovies.

To understand the significance of this warming effect, take a few moments now to conduct the following scientific experiment in your bathroom. First, fill your bathtub with water and note the temperature. Now mix in these ingredients: 25 pounds of salt, to simulate the ocean's salinity; one 12-ounce can of Bumble Bee brand chunk light tuna, to simulate the ocean's marine life; and one plastic Ken doll wearing a dark suit, to simulate Vice President Gore.

Now, using a standard household blowtorch, gradually heat the water while swishing it around the tub in a counterclockwise direction. Do you see what's happening? That's correct: A big old ugly greasy wad of hair has broken loose from the drain and is bobbing toward you like a hostile mutant marine tarantula. This is exactly what is happening in the Pacific Ocean, except that the hair wad is more than one million times larger. The only thing comparable to it on land is Donald Trump.

So we can see why El Niño has the scientific community so alarmed. The question is, what is causing it? What widespread phenomenon has occurred lately that would make a major ocean suddenly start warming up? The answer, according to a recent scientific study by the

Institute of Scientists Who Have Done Studies Recently, is: espresso machines. A few years ago, you hardly ever saw these machines; now they're showing up in Dairy Queens. These are not energy-efficient devices. For every ounce of actual espresso they produce, they release enough steam into the atmosphere to meet the energy needs of Finland for a year.

This is not to say that espresso is the sole cause of El Niño. Other recent trends that probably play a part are cigar smoking, line dancing, nostril rings, and those incomprehensible commercials for something called "Lucent." We need to ban all of these things immediately, and as a precautionary measure we should also evacuate the West Coast as far inland as Nebraska. If you care at all about the environment, you will write to your congresshuman and demand that something be done immediately. And then you will clean your bathtub.

Pine Sap Transfusions Could Save Your Christmas Tree's Life

Today's holiday topic is: Christmas Tree Care.

The Christmas tree is a cherished holiday tradition that dates back 500 years, to the early Germans. What happened was, one night right around Christmas, a bunch of early Germans were sitting around, and one of them, named Helmut, said: "I know! Let's chop down a perfectly good fir tree, drag it inside, and see if we can get it to stand up again!"

"Why in the world would we do THAT?" asked the other early Germans, who also happened to speak English.

"It's a cherished holiday tradition!" replied Helmut.

This made sense to the other Germans, because they had just invented beer. So they went out, chopped down a tree, dragged it home, and spent the next four days trying to make it stand up. We now know that, under the laws of physics, this is impossible. Nevertheless, the tradition of trying to erect Christmas trees continues to the present day. We should be grateful that the early Germans didn't decide to drag home some large forest organism that is even LESS appropriate for interior use than a tree. Imagine what Christmas would be like today if they had used, for example, a moose. We'd have millions of families driving home with a dead Christmas moose strapped to the roof of the car; and then Dad would spend hours trying to get the moose to fit into a cheesy $4.99 drugstore moose stand; and then the whole family would decorate it; and then, as everybody gathered around in admiration, it would topple majestically to the ground. So it would be essentially the same as what we do now, except that Dad would not get pine sap in his hair.

But the point is that the Christmas tree is a cherished tradition, as reflected in the lyrics to the classic Christmas carol "O Tannenbaum":

> *O Tannenbaum, O Tannenbaum,*
> *Something something something,*
> *So bring us some figgy pudding,*
> *But not TOO figgy, because we get gas.*

Now let's talk about caring for your Christmas tree. According to the American Association of Guys Without All Their Teeth Selling Christmas Trees From Tents, the major varieties of Christmas tree are: Pine, Spruce, Douglas Fir, Walnut, Fake, Balsa, and Douglas Firbanks Jr. The Association recommends that, before you buy a tree, you should always have Dad pick it up and bang it hard on the ground a couple of times; according to the Association, this is "a lot of fun to watch."

Once you get the tree home and set up in its stand (allow six to eight weeks) you will want to take measures to prevent it from shedding needles all over your floor. The best way to do this, according to the Association, is to "remove your floor." If that is not practical, you can make a mixture of four cups of water, two tablespoons of bleach, and one tablespoon of sugar, but it will do you no good. When decorating the tree, always use strings of cheap lights manufactured in Third

World nations that only recently found out about electricity. Shop around for light strings that have been presnarled at the factory for your convenience.

OK! Now that we've covered tree care, it's time for this: SPECIAL HOLIDAY SAFETY TIP: If you're staging a Nativity show, and you're thinking of using live animals, you had best think again. This tip is based on an alarming newspaper story from the December 23, 1997, issue of the Annapolis, Maryland, *Capital,* written by Christopher Munsey and sent in by alert reader Katie Gibbs (other reports of the same incident were sent by George Spilich).

The *Capital* story, which I swear I am not making up, is headlined: "Huge Camel Fleeing Live Nativity Scene Killed on Route 50." It states that on the night of Sunday, December 21, a church was preparing to stage a Nativity show featuring live animals, when a six-foot-tall, 600-pound camel named Ernie escaped, ran onto a highway, was struck by a car, and went to That Big Zoo in the Sky. The article quotes the driver of the car that hit Ernie as saying: "How in the hell is a camel on Route 50 in the United States of America?"

These are words that we would all be wise to remember. But let us not let the threat of colliding with escaped camels dampen the joy we feel during this special time of year, as expressed in the traditional carol "Deck the Halls":

> *Deck the halls with boughs of holly!*
> *Fa la la la la, la la la (crash)*

Don't Eat the Muskrats or the Poinsettia au Gratin

We have some important news for those of you who have been harboring an urge to eat poinsettias. This news comes from an article in the December 5, 1999, edition of the Harrisburg, Pennsylvania, *Patriot-News*, sent in by alert reader Karen Durkin. The article makes this fascinating statement:

> Despite persistent rumors, poinsettias are NOT poisonous. Ohio State University testing has found that a 50-pound child could eat more than 500 poinsettia bracts with no ill effects other than possibly a sick stomach from eating that much foliage.

The two questions that immediately come to mind are:

1. What is a "bract"?
2. Would "Bill and the Bracts" be a good name for a rock band?

(Answers: 1. Part of a plant; 2. No, but "The Foliage Eaters" would.)

Another question is: How did Ohio State University conduct this research? Did researchers actually feed 500 poinsettia bracts to a 50-pound child? How? ("Eat your bracts, Jason, or NO MORE POKÉMON CARDS FOR YOU!") And does this experiment really prove that poinsettias are safe? We personally have seen 50-pound children eat a LOT of things that would probably kill an adult, such as "Fruit Roll-Ups," which we do not believe are fruit at all. We believe they are the offspring of a biological mating experiment involving Kool-Aid and flypaper.

So our feeling is that you consumers should resist the temptation to rush out and start wolfing down poinsettias. Instead, you should take the wise scientific precaution of serving them to dinner guests ("Marge, try some of this delicious brie-on-a-bract!") and then watching the guests closely for common symptoms of death, such as not moving for several days, or purchasing an Oldsmobile.

But here's what really gets our goat: While so-called "researchers" at Ohio State University were busily stuffing poinsettias down the throat of an innocent 50-pound child, a potentially MUCH greater menace to humanity was running loose in the very same state (Ohio). We know this because we have received, from an anonymous source who shall remain nameless, a newspaper article from the October 29, 1999, edition of the Youngstown, Ohio, *Vindicator*, which bills itself—and not without reason—as the premier newspaper in the Mahoning Valley. This article, which we are not making up, begins with the following statement:

WARREN—The possibility that radioactive musk-rats are lurking in the city bothers Pierson "Butch" Butcher Jr.

The article states that Butcher, an unsuccessful Republican candidate for the Warren City Council, had said it was possible that local muskrats were eating radioactive materials they found on the grounds of a recently demolished power plant. By way of rebuttal, the story quotes the mayor, Democrat Hank Angelo, as stating: "There are no green, glowing-eyed rats running the streets of Warren."

In professional journalism, the first thing we do when we need to check out this type of story is try to find out what a muskrat is. The sum total of our knowledge on this subject is the song "Muskrat Love," performed by The Captain and Tennille, both of whom are, incredibly, still at large. So we checked the encyclopedia, which states that muskrats are "closely related to voles." We have never heard of "voles," and suspect that the encyclopedia is just kidding around.

Armed with this information, we called Warren, Ohio, and spoke with Pierson "Butch" Butcher Jr., who, it turns out, is not a shy person. During a lengthy and wide-ranging interview, he stated that although there are muskrats running around Warren, and SOMEBODY at a public meeting expressed concern that they (the muskrats) might be radioactive, that person was not Pierson "Butch" Butcher Jr. Mr. Butcher further stated that he had read an article somewhere regarding reports of radioactive deer in Pennsylvania.

So to summarize the key findings of our investigation:

1. There may or may not be radioactive muskrats and/or deer in Ohio and/or Pennsylvania.
2. Just in case, both of these states should be evacuated immediately.
3. Another good name for a band would be "The Radioactive Muskrats."
4. Speaking of musical groups, if The Captain and

Tennille ever decide to try for a comeback, the obvious song for them to do would be "Vole Love."
5. In which case, please pass the poinsettias.

Everything I Know About Dieting
I Learned on *Leeza*

One recent Tuesday morning I was flipping through the
TV channels at a brisk, business-like, no-nonsense pace,
looking for *Rocky and Bullwinkle*, when I found myself
caught up in a fascinating installment of Leeza Gibbons'
talk show, *Leeza*. The theme of the show was: "Women
Who Cannot Correctly Spell Their Own Names."

No, seriously, the theme was: "Superstars of the Diet

Wars." This was a debate among top diet experts, who felt so strongly about the correct way to lose weight that at times they came close to whacking each other over the head with their competing diet books.

Dieting was not always so complicated. Thousands of years ago, there was only one diet book, entitled *Don't Eat Too Much*. It consisted of a big stone tablet on which were chiseled the words "DON'T EAT TOO MUCH!" It did not sell well, because nobody could lift it, on top of which everybody back then was busy with other concerns, such as not starving.

In modern America, however, food is abundant everywhere except aboard commercial airplanes. Dieting has become a huge industry involving many complex theories that can be confusing to the average layperson sitting on the Barcalounger, trying to decide whether to open a second bag of potato chips or simply eat the onion dip right out of the tub. So let's review the History of Modern Diet Science:

The first big advance came 1895, when a food researcher named Dr. Wilbur Calorie made the breakthrough discovery, while working late one night, that he could no longer pull his pants up past his thighs. After spending many hours in the laboratory squinting at fudge, Dr. Calorie concluded that people gain weight because certain foods contain tiny invisible scientific units that became known, in honor of their discoverer, as "Wilburs."

No, sorry, I mean "calories." For decades, everybody operated on the Calorie Counter Theory of dieting, which basically states that you should never eat anything that tastes good. Then along came a new theory, the Evil Fat Theory, which states that you CAN have calories, but you should NOT have fat; this resulted in the multibillion-dollar Low-Fat Things Industry, which gave us low-fat brownies, low-fat Milk Duds, low-fat cows, low-fat cologne, the cast of *Friends,* etc.

But there is ANOTHER major theory that says you can eat all the fat you want, but you CAN'T have carbohydrates; that you can snork down an entire pig for breakfast, but eat a single Froot Loop and you will bloat out like a military life raft. The Evil Carbohydrate Theory is extremely hot at the moment, as is evidenced by the top-selling diet books, which include *Carbohydrate Beaters, Carbohydrate Busters, Carbohydrate Whackers, Let's Poke Carbohydrates in the Eyeball, Carbohydrates Kidnapped My Wife,* and *Fight Carbohydrates Through Sorcery the Harry Potter Way.*

So it's hard for a dieter to know what to think, which is why it was so helpful for the *Leeza* show to hold a debate among the leading diet experts, including several medical doctors, several people with scientific initials after their names, and of course Suzanne Somers, who may yet win a Nobel Prize for her work on the Thigh-Master, and who is now a top diet authority with a book out. It is only a matter of time before she thinks seriously about running for president.

So anyway, the diet experts debated their theories, and Leeza walked around frowning with the deep concern that talk-show hosts feel about everything. The audience provided feedback by holding up cards that said YES on one side and NO on the other. (At one point an expert mentioned the first law of thermodynamics, and Leeza asked if anybody knew what that was, and the audience consensus was NO.) In between there were numerous commercials, most of which were for law firms that want to Fight For You, although there was also a thought-provoking one for a toilet cleanser.

Anyway, I watched the experts debate for an hour, and here's what I learned:

- The (pick one: low-calorie; low-fat; low-carbohydrate) diet really works!
- Whereas the (pick one: low-calorie; low-fat; low-carbohydrate) diet will probably kill you.
- Suzanne Somers, in all objectivity, thinks you should buy her book.
- If you are a human being of any kind, you should file a lawsuit, because YOU HAVE MONEY COMING!
- Speaking of TV attorneys, toilet bacteria grow like CRAZY.

So there are the facts, consumers; it's now up to you to make an informed decision. Remember: It's YOUR body. And, as such, it wants a chili dog.

The Banzai Chef

Today's culinary topic is: How to Make Sushi

I happen to be an expert on this topic because I recently put in a stint as a chef at an actual sushi restaurant. (One of the first things you learn, as a sushi chef, is how to put in a stint.)

Before I give you the details, I should explain, for the benefit of those of you who live in remote wilderness regions such as Iowa, what sushi is. Basically, it is a type of cuisine developed by the Japanese as part of an ancient tradition of seeing what is the scariest thing they can get you to eat raw.

The way they do this is, they start out by serving you a nice, non-threatening piece of fish, from which all the identifying fish parts have been removed. This fish is safe to eat and tasty. But the trick is that it's served with a green condiment called "wasabi," which is the Japanese word for "nuclear horseradish." This is an extremely spicy substance, the formula for which must never be allowed to fall into the hands of Saddam Hussein. If you put more than two wasabi molecules on your sushi and eat it, your hair will burst into flames.

So after consuming some wasabi, you naturally order a cool refreshing Japanese beer to pour on your head and perhaps, since you have the bottle in your hand anyway, wet your whistle with. The result is that your judgment becomes impaired, which is when they start trying to get you to eat prank food, such as sea-urchin eggs. Sea urchins are vicious, golf-ball-shaped, poison-spined sea creatures whose sole ecological purpose is to ruin your tropical vacation by deliberately not getting out of your way when you are wading barefoot. If you eat the eggs of this animal, and fail to chew them thoroughly, you could develop an alarming medical condition that doctors call "baby sea urchins walking around inside your body poking holes in your spleen."

Other prank foods that they will try to get you to eat at sushi bars include eels, clam parts, jellyfish, tentacles with flagrant suckers, and shrimps with their eyeballs still waving around on stalks. If you eat those, the waiter will become brazen and start bringing out chunks of coral and live electric eels. My point is that, in a sushi restaurant, you must watch carefully what you eat (this is exactly what "The Star-Spangled Banner" is referring to when it says "o'er the clam parts we watched").

Despite this, I happen to be a big fan of non-prank sushi. And so when Bok An, the proprietor of Sakura, my local sushi restaurant in Coral Gables, invited me to be a guest sushi chef, I enthusiastically answered: "No!" I was afraid that I'd have to touch an eel. I am 51 years old, and I did not get this far by touching eels.

But Bok assured me that we would stick to basic fish species such as tuna, salmon, and cucumber. And thus I found myself one Tuesday night, wearing a samurai-style headband and standing behind the sushi bar, blending in perfectly with the other sushi chefs, except that my headband was actually the belt of my bathrobe.

Bok stood next to me and prepared various sushi items, and I attempted to imitate him. Here's the recipe: You start with a little rectangle made of dried seaweed (I asked Bok where the seaweed comes from, thinking he would name some ancient Japanese seaside village, and he said, "a distributor"). Then you pick up a glob of special sticky rice and spread it evenly on the seaweed. At least Bok did. The majority of my rice remained firmly stuck to my hands and started migrating to other parts of my body. I may have to have it removed surgically.

Next, you cut up your ingredients, using a lethal-looking, extremely sharp sushi knife that causes professional sushi chefs to become very nervous when it is being wielded by a professional humor columnist. Then you put these ingredients on the rice and execute the secret sushi-rolling technique, which is difficult to describe in English words, as we can see by this actual transcript of Bok explaining it to me: "OK, you go like this, Boom! Then you go, Boom! Boom! Boom!"

The thing was, when Bok went boom, he produced this attractive, appetizing cylinder of sushi. Whereas when I went boom, I produced this mutant food unit leaking random seafood parts. I also had a problem with my sizing: Sushi rolls are supposed to be small, bite-size morsels; mine were more along the lines of seaweed-covered hams.

But I kept trying. Remember the movie *Karate Kid*, where the mean bully beats up Ralph Macchio, but then Ralph studies karate under Mr. Miyagi, and then finally, in the big tournament, with everybody watching, Ralph stuns the bully by rolling a reasonably tight cucumber roll? Well, that's what I did. In fact, I may have a knack for it. So if one day you walk into a Japanese restaurant, and you see, standing behind the sushi bar, what appears to be a man-size blob of rice wearing a blue bathrobe belt on its head, feel free to say hi. But keep your distance if I'm holding a knife.

Turkey Day

So this year, you agreed to host the big family Thanksgiving dinner. Congratulations! You moron!

No, seriously, hosting Thanksgiving dinner does NOT have to be traumatic. The key is planning. For example, every year my family spends Thanksgiving at the home of a friend named Arlene Reidy, who prepares dinner for a huge number of people. I can't give an exact figure, because my eyeballs become fogged with gravy. But I'm pretty sure that Arlene is feeding several branches of the armed forces.

And Arlene is not slapping just any old food on the table, either. She's a gourmet cook who can make anything. I bet she has a recipe for cold fusion. She serves moist, tender turkeys the size of Arnold Schwarzenegger, accompanied by a vast array of exotic hors d'oeuvres and 350 kinds of sweet potatoes made from scratch. I'm pretty sure Arlene threshes her own wheat.

If you were to look into Arlene's dining room at the end of Thanksgiving dinner, it would at first appear to be empty. Then you'd hear groans and burps coming from under the table, and you'd realize that the guests, no longer able to cope with the food and gravity at the same time, were lying on the floor. Every now and then you'd see a hand snake up over the edge of the table, grab a handful of stuffing, then dart back under the table again,

182

after which you'd hear chewing, then swallowing, then the sound of digestive organs rupturing. Some guests have to be rushed by ambulance to the hospital, receiving pumpkin pie intravenously en route.

The question is: How is Arlene able to prepare such an amazing feast for so many people? The answer is simple: I have no idea. I'm always watching football when it happens. But my point is that, if you want to provide your Thanksgiving guests with a delicious home-cooked meal, one approach would be to go to Arlene's house and steal some of her food when she's busy churning the butter. She'd never notice. She has enough leftovers to make turkey sandwiches for everybody in Belgium.

If you prefer to do your own cooking this Thanksgiving, your first step is to calculate how much turkey you need. Home economists tell us that the average 155-pound person consumes 1.5 pounds of turkey, so if you're planning to have 14 relatives for dinner, you'd simply multiply 14 times 1.5 times 155, which means your turkey should weigh, let's see, carry the two . . . 3,255 pounds. If you can't find a turkey that size, you should call up selected relatives and explain to them, in a sensitive and diplomatic manner, that they can't come because they weigh too much.

In selecting a turkey, remember that the fresher it is, the better it will taste. That's why, if you go into the kitchen of top professional homemaker Martha Stewart on Thanksgiving morning, you'll find her whacking a live turkey with a hatchet. In fact, you'll find Martha doing this *every* morning.

"It just relaxes me," she reports.

Your other option is to get a frozen turkey at the supermarket. The Turkey Manufacturers Association recommends that, before you purchase a frozen bird, you check it for firmness by test-dropping it on the super-market floor—it should bounce three vertical inches per pound—and then take a core sample of the breast by drilling into it with a $3/8$-inch masonry bit until you strike the giblets. If supermarket employees attempt to question you, the Turkey Manufacturers Association recommends that you "gesture at them with the drill in a reassuring manner."

When you get the turkey home, you should thaw it completely by letting it sit on a standard kitchen counter at room temperature for one half of the turkey's weight in hours, or roughly 19 weeks. "If you see spiders nesting in your turkey," states the Turkey Manufacturers Association, "you waited too long."

Once the turkey is defrosted, you simply cook it in a standard household oven at 138.4 degrees centimeter for 27 minutes per pound (29 minutes for married taxpayers filing jointly). Add four minutes for each 100 feet of your home's elevation above sea level, which you should determine using a standard household sextant. Inspect the turkey regularly as it cooks; when you notice that the skin has started to blister, the time has come for you to give your guests the message they've been eagerly awaiting: "Run!" Because you left the plastic wrapper on the turkey, and it's about to explode, spewing out flaming salmonella units at the speed of sound.

As you stand outside waiting for the fire trucks, you should take a moment to count your blessings. The main one, of course, is that you will definitely *not* be asked to host the big family Thanksgiving dinner next year. But it's also important to remember—as our Pilgrim forepar-ents remembered on the very first Thanksgiving—that two excellent names for rock bands would be "The Turkey Spiders" and "The Flaming Salmonella Units."

Independence Day

This year, why not hold an old-fashioned Fourth of July Picnic?

Food poisoning is one good reason. After a few hours in the sun, ordinary potato salad can develop bacteria the size of raccoons. But don't let the threat of agonizingly painful death prevent you from celebrating the birth of our nation, just as Americans have been doing ever since that historic first July Fourth when our Founding Fathers—George Washington, Benjamin Franklin, Thomas Jefferson, Bob Dole, and Tony Bennett—landed on Plymouth Rock.

Step one in planning your picnic is to decide on a menu. Martha Stewart has loads of innovative suggestions for unique, imaginative, and tasty summer meals. So you can forget about her. "If Martha Stewart comes anywhere near my picnic, she's risking a barbecue fork to the eyeball" should be your patriotic motto. Because you're having a *traditional* Fourth of July picnic, and that means a menu of hot dogs charred into cylinders of industrial-grade carbon, and hamburgers so undercooked that when people try to eat them, they leap off the plate and frolic on the lawn like otters.

Dad should be in charge of the cooking, because only Dad, being a male of the masculine gender, has the mechanical "know-how" to operate a piece of technology as complex as a barbecue grill. To be truly traditional, the grill should be constructed of the following materials:

—4 percent "rust-resistant" steel;
—58 percent rust;
—23 percent hardened black grill scunge from food cooked as far back as 1987 (the scunge should never be scraped off, because it is what is actually holding the grill together);
—15 percent spiders.

If the grill uses charcoal as a fuel, Dad should remember to start lighting the fire early (no later than April 10) because charcoal, in accordance with federal safety regulations, is a mineral that does not burn. The spiders get a huge kick out of watching Dad attempt to ignite it; they emit hearty spider chuckles and slap themselves on all eight knees. This is why many dads prefer the modern gas grill, which ignites at the press of a button and burns with a steady, even flame until you put food on it, at which time it runs out of gas.

While Dad is saying traditional bad words to the barbecue grill, Mom can organize the kids for a fun activity: making old-fashioned ice cream by hand, the way our grandparents' generation did. You'll need a hand-cranked ice-cream maker, which you can pick up at any antique store for $1,875. All you do is put in the ingredients, and start cranking! It makes no difference what specific ingredients you put in, because—I speak from bitter experience here—no matter how long you crank them, they will never, ever turn into ice cream. Scientists laugh at the very concept. "Ice cream is not formed by cranking," they point out. "Ice cream is formed by freezers." Our grandparents' generation wasted millions of man-hours trying to produce ice cream by hand; this is what caused the Great Depression.

When the kids get tired of trying to make ice cream (allow about 25 seconds for this) it's time to play some traditional July Fourth games. One of the most popular is the "sack race." All you need is a bunch of old-fashioned burlap sacks, which you can obtain from the J. Peterman catalog for $227.50 apiece. Call the kids outside, have them line up on the lawn, and give each one a sack to climb into; then shout "GO!" and watch the hilarious antics begin as, one by one, the kids sneak back indoors and resume trying to locate pornography on the Internet.

Come nightfall, though, everybody will be drawn back outside by the sound of loud, traditional Fourth of July explosions coming from all around the neighborhood. These are caused by the fact that various dads, after consuming a number of traditionally fermented beverages, have given up on conventional charcoal-lighting products and escalated to gasoline. As the spectacular pyrotechnic show lights up the night sky, you begin to truly appreciate the patriotic meaning of the words to "The Star-Spangled Banner," written by Francis Scott Key to commemorate the fledgling nation's first barbecue:

> And the grill parts' red glare;
> Flaming spiders in air;
> Someone call 911;
> There's burning scunge in Dad's hair

After the traditional visit to the hospital emergency room, it's time to gather 'round and watch Uncle Bill set off the fireworks that he purchased from a roadside stand operated by people who spend way more on tattoos than dental hygiene. As Uncle Bill lights the firework fuse and scurries away, everybody is on pins and needles until, suddenly and dramatically, the fuse goes out. So Uncle Bill re-lights the fuse and scurries away again, and the fuse goes out again, and so on, with Uncle Bill scurrying back and forth with his Bic lighter like a deranged Olympic torchbearer until, finally, the fuse burns all the way down, and the firework, emitting a smoke puff the size of a grapefruit, makes a noise—"phut"—like a squirrel passing gas. Wow! What a fitting climax for your traditional old-fashioned July Fourth picnic!

Next year you'll go out for Chinese food.

High-Fivin', Bosom-Ogling Soccer Lizard Must Die!

The only time I got really scared was when the mob surrounded me and began beating on my head. Fortunately, it was not my usual head: It was the head of a giant lizard.

I was wearing the giant-lizard head because—and this is why people who value their dignity should avoid journalism—I thought it would be fun to write about being a sports-team mascot and engaging in comical hijinks with the crowd. The mascot that I wound up being is named "P.K.," which stands for "Penalty Kick." P.K., a seven-foot green lizard, is the mascot for the Miami Fusion, a professional soccer team of which I'm a big fan.

I like soccer because there's a lot of action and drama. There are no time-outs, so the only way players can catch their breath is to sustain a major injury, which some of them are very good at. A guy will get bumped by another player, or a beam of sunlight, and he'll hurl himself dramatically to the ground, writhing and clutching his leg (not necessarily the leg that got bumped) and screaming that the referee should get a priest out there immediately to administer the last rites, or at least call a foul. The referee generally ignores the player, who, after a while, gets up and continues playing. Some players

189

suffer four or five fatal injuries per game. That's how tough they are.

Here's another example of soccer-player toughness, which I am not making up: Last year, in Brazil, there was a soccer match between two arch-rival teams, one of which is nicknamed "The Rabbits." The other team scored a goal, and the guy who scored it celebrated by reaching into his shorts, pulling out a carrot, and eating it. He had a carrot in his shorts the whole time! Talk about team spirit! You wonder what he'd do if he played a team nicknamed "The Eel Eaters."

But back to my point: I asked Fusion officials if I could wear the P.K. costume at a game, and they said OK. And so one Sunday afternoon I found myself in an office next to the stadium, struggling into the P.K. out-fit, which includes green leggings, green arms with only four fingers per hand, big feet, a four-foot tail, and a large lizard head with buggy eyes and a grinning, snouty mouth. Helping me put these items on was the regular Fusion mascot, Tony Mozzott, who, when he is not a giant lizard, manages a supermarket meat department. As he attached my tail, Tony gave me some mascotting tips, such as: "I high-five people, because if you shake their hands, they'll try to take off your fingers."

Finally I was suited up, and, with Tony guiding me, I waddled into the stadium. I wish you could have seen the crowd reaction. I wish I could have seen it, too. But it turns out that—biologists, take note—lizards actually see through their mouths, and my mouth was pointing down at a 45-degree angle, so all I could see was legs and small children. I saw a lot of children. They love to run directly into mascots at full speed, and they tend to hit you right where you'd carry your carrot, if you catch my drift.

Keeping a wary eye out for incoming tots, I moved slowly and blindly around the stadium, pausing every now and then to wave at the crowd, enthusiastically and totally cluelessly, exactly like a U.S. presidential candidate. It was going pretty well until I wandered into the stadium end zone, where a group of hard-core soccer fans hang out. Going there was a bad idea for two reasons: (1) Serious soccer purists are not fond of the mascot concept; and (2) The opposing team had just scored a goal. So the mood in the hard-core zone was unhappy.

Of course P.K. the lizard did not know any of this. P.K. was just shuffling along, a big, blind, green, high-fivin', wavin' wad of fun. My first inkling of trouble came when man stuck his face deep into my mouth opening and made a very uncomplimentary remark. Hoping to win him over via hijinks, I attempted to high-five him, but somebody grabbed me, and then somebody else yanked on my tail, and within seconds there were people all around me, shouting and grabbing and pounding on my head. It was like being inside the bass drum at a Metallica concert.

The problem with being a mascot in this situation is that you have no way to indicate distress: Your mascot face keeps right on smiling happily. But believe me, the inner lizard was scared. Fortunately, Tony and some security guards quickly came to my rescue, and the remainder of my stint as mascot went smoothly. The rest of the crowd seemed friendly; I high-fived and waved at a lot of invisible people. I also noted one interesting fact: If you're wearing a lizard costume, and a woman walks up and stands right in front of you, you are looking, through the lizard's mouth, directly at the female attributes that women are always accusing guys of looking at. You can't help it! But the woman cannot tell, because the eyeballs on your mascot head appear to be making mature eye contact with her.

I pass this fact along for you guys who are pondering a career in the giant-lizard field. My advice is, stay out of the end zone. And wear a cup.

Build Yourself a Killer Bod with Killer Bees

If there's one ideal that unites all Americans, it's the belief that every single one of us, regardless of ethnic background, is fat.

It was not always this way. There was a time, not so long ago, when Americans did not obsess about fat. In those days, a man could be portly and still be considered attractive. The standards were also more lenient for women: Marilyn Monroe, whom nobody ever called skinny, was a major sex goddess.

By today's beauty standards, of course, Marilyn Monroe was an oil tanker. Today's beauty ideal, strictly enforced by the media, is a person with the same level of body fat as a paper clip. Turn on your TV, and all you see are men and women who would rather have both eyeballs removed via corkscrew than eat a slice of pizza. These are genetic mutants: You can see their muscles, veins, and neck bones almost bursting through their fat-free skin. I don't know who decided that the see-through look was attractive; I, personally, have never heard anybody express lust for anybody else's internal organs. But we normal humans are constantly exposed to the zero-fat mutants in the media, and we naturally assume that we're supposed to look like them. This is of course impossible, but we try. We diet constantly, especially young women, many of whom now start dieting while still in the womb.

And of course we spend millions of dollars on "exercise," defined as "activity designed to be strenuous without accomplishing anything useful." For example, we drive our cars to health clubs so we can run on treadmills. But we do NOT run to the health club, because then we would be accomplishing something useful. We pedal furiously on exercise bicycles that do not go anywhere. We take elevators every chance we get, but we buy expensive machines that enable us to pretend we're climbing stairs. It would not surprise me if yuppies started paying potato farmers for the opportunity to go into the fields and burn fat by pretending to conduct a harvest, taking great care not to dig up any actual potatoes.

If you think that's ridiculous, then you haven't seen "Tae-Bo." This is the current hot fad, advertised extensively on TV by perspiring mutants. As I understand it, Tae-Bo is based on martial arts; the difference is that martial artists actually learn to defend themselves, whereas Tae-Bo people throw pretend punches and kicks strictly for fitness purposes. While they're busy kicking air and checking their abdominals, an actual mugger could walk right up and whack them with a crowbar.

But never mind practicality. The point is that right now Tae-Bo is very, very hot, which means that soon everybody will get bored with it. That's what always happens with exercise trends: People realize that, after countless hours of pretending to climb stairs or punching the air, they still bear a stronger resemblance to the Michelin Tire Man than to the TV mutants. So they give up on that particular trend and look for a new one.

Will this craziness ever end? Will Americans ever

come to their senses and stop wasting millions and millions of dollars on hopeless efforts to look like people who don't really look like people? I hope not, because I'm planning to cash in on this. I got my idea from a wonderful newspaper article, sent in by alert veterinarian Steven Berry, from the April 7, 1999, edition of the *Leader News* of Central City, Kentucky. The article, written by Paul Camplin, is headlined "Cobbs Invented Odd Sport of Bee Fighting as Family Entertainment." It concerns the descendants of Bunn and Betty Cobb of Calhoun, Kentucky, who have gotten together annually for about 70 years to fight wild bees for fun. The article states:

"Without use of protective gear, one of the group approaches the bumble-bee hive and whacks it with a stick. When all of the now angry bees come flying out the group of bee fighters simply fight off the bees as best they can with large clumps of maple leaves."

The article, which I am not making up, is illustrated by photos of members of the extended Cobb family, including grandparents, wildly waving branches at bees.

When I saw those photos, I knew I was looking at a gold mine. I'm talking about the Next Big Fitness Trend: "Tae-Bee." I'm going to make a 30-minute TV infomercial wherein enthusiastic hired mutants stress the benefits of bee-fighting (". . . and while you're OUCH burning fat, your arm motion is also OUCH building those OUCH . . .").

In no time millions of Americans will be ordering the Tae-Bee workout videotape, along with the Official (Accept No Substitutes!) Tae-Bee Maple Leaf Clump and of course the Official Tae-Bee Box o' Really Mad Bees. And if you don't think Americans will pay good money to get stung, I have one word for you: "Thigh-Master."

So laugh if you want: I'm going to get rich on this thing. And then I'm going to hire a personal trainer. His sole job will be to order my pizza.

High-Tech Twinkie Wars Will Be No Picnic

I'll tell you when I start to worry. I start to worry when "officials" tell me not to worry. This is why I am very concerned about the following Associated Press report, which was sent to me by a number of alert readers:

> RICHLAND, WASH.—Radioactive ants, flies and gnats have been found at the Hanford nuclear complex, bringing to mind those Cold-War-era "B" horror movies in which giant mutant insects are the awful price paid for mankind's entry into the Atomic Age.
>
> Officials at the nation's most contaminated nuclear site insist there is no danger of Hanford becoming the setting for a '90s version of *Them!*, the 1954 movie starring James Arness and James Whitmore in which huge, marauding ants are spawned by nuclear experiments in the desert.

Should we trust these "officials"? I'll let you decide for yourself what the answer is (NO). But consider:

- For years, "officials" insisted that our cars needed air bags for safety; then, when we GOT air bags, "officials" started warning us how dangerous they are, the result being that many concerned parents now strap their children to the car roof.

- For years, "officials" told us that marijuana was an evil criminal drug. Now they tell us that it has "important medical benefits warranting further investigation, but first let's order a pizza."
- Every year, "officials" tell us to turn all our clocks ahead one hour, only to turn around a few months later and tell us to turn them BACK. Make up your minds, "officials"!

My point is that we cannot trust "officials" any farther than we can throw them by the leg. This is especially true when it comes to the Hanford nuclear complex. When this complex was built, "officials" said it was safe; now the whole area glows like a Budweiser sign. So when "officials" tell us that the radioactive Hanford insects are NOT going to mutate into giant monsters like the ants depicted in the 1954 movie *Them!*, it clearly is time to study this movie and see what happened, because it is about to happen again.

I did not see *Them!,* but I do have a plot summary from a book called *Guide for the Film Fanatic.* It states that after James Whitmore and James Arness discover the giant mutant ants marauding around the New Mexico desert, they kill most of them by burning their nest; however, some ants escape, and the heroes "trace them to Los Angeles." The book doesn't say why the heroes would have to "trace" the ants; you'd think that if marauding insects the size of houses showed up in a heavily populated area, it would be mentioned prominently in the news media, but *Guide for the Film Fanatic* makes it sound as though Arness and Whitmore had to track the ants down via detective techniques:

JAMES ARNESS (*showing a photograph to a store-keeper*): Have you seen this ant? It's 23 feet tall.

STOREKEEPER (frowning at the photograph): Hmmm . . .
We did have a 40-foot praying mantis in here last
week, but I don't recall any . . . Wait a minute!
Aren't you Marshal Dillon from Gunsmoke?
JAMES ARNESS: Not until 1955.

Anyway, the heroes finally locate the giant ants in the
Los Angeles sewer system, where, according to *Guide for
the Film Fanatic*, there is "a thrilling finale." The *Guide*
gives no details on this finale, so we don't know whether
the ants are killed, or mutate again and become agents,
or what.

But the point is this: If, as now seems likely, the
radioactive insects at the Hanford complex mutate and
start marauding, they will almost certainly head for Los
Angeles. This is a terrifying prospect. Imagine how you
would feel if you tuned in to the evening news and
learned that, for example, Fran Drescher had been sucked
dry by a gnat the size of a water buffalo. You'd feel
pretty excited. You'd hope there was video.

But innocent people could also be hurt, and that is
why we need to take action NOW. Instead of frittering
away billions on this *Star Wars* missile-defense system,
we need to use that money to construct, in the desert
outside of Los Angeles, a 100-foot-high, 500-foot-long,
fully functional Hostess Twinkie. The giant insects would
be attracted to the Twinkie, and while they were munch-
ing on it, an Earth-orbiting manned space station would
launch a rocket-propelled, laser-guided, nine-story-high,
18,000-pound man's shoe, which would, by the time it
reached the Twinkie, be traveling at over 6,000 miles
per hour, resulting in a Stomp of Doom that would hurl
globs of cream filling as far as St. Louis.

Of course building a weapons system this size would
not be easy. There would be political considerations:

Powerful members of Congress would insist on having giant Twinkies built in their states, too. But that is a small price to pay for national security. We must proceed with this! We already have the technology! Which means, of course, that so does China.

Be an Internet Millionaire, and
We May Like You

Everybody—by which I mean "not you"—is getting rich off the Internet. We are constantly seeing stories in the media about young Internet entrepreneurs who look like they should be mowing lawns for spending money, except that they have the same net worth as Portugal. Six months ago, they were college students, sitting around their dorms, trying to figure out what body part to pierce next; now they're the CEOs of Something-Dot-Com, and they're buying mansions, jets, camels, etc., not to mention van Gogh and Renoir (I'm not talking about their paintings; I'm talking about their actual *corpses*).

When we read about these spectacularly successful young people—who, through their boldness and vision, have realized the American Dream, and in so doing have created the greatest economic boom the world has ever seen, thereby benefiting all of us—we cannot help but express our gratitude as follows: "I hope they get leprosy."

No! We must not be petty and jealous, just because these people are young AND rich. Instead we must philosophically ask ourselves: "Are these young zillionaires truly *happy*? Does all that money really give them any more pleasure than I can get from simply watching a sunrise, or chatting with an old friend?"

You cretin: Of COURSE it does. These people are so

rich that, if they want, they can install giant hydraulic hoists under the entire horizon, so they can raise it up and watch the same sunrise TWICE. And they can buy all the old friends they want. They can buy YOUR old friends. When you ask your old friends to come over and chat, they'll say, "Sorry! I've been invited to a 22-year-old zillionaire's house to watch him raise the horizon!"

So the bottom line is, if you want to be happy in today's economy, you need to be rich, too. This means that you have to become involved with the Internet, which has brought about the most revolutionary change in business communications since 1876, when the great inventor Alexander Graham Bell first figured out how to make callers on hold listen to Barry Manilow.

What, exactly, is the Internet? Basically it is a global network exchanging digitized data in such a way that any computer, anywhere, that is equipped with a device called a "modem," can make a noise like a duck choking on a kazoo. This is called "logging on," and once you are "logged on," you can move the "pointer" of your "mouse" to a "hyperlink," and simply by "clicking" on it, change your "pointer" to an "hourglass." Then you can go to "lunch," and when you come back, there, on your computer screen, as if by magic, will be at least 14 advertisements related to Beanie Babies (which currently are the foundation of the entire world economy). This entire process takes place in less time than it takes for a sperm whale to give birth to twins.

The business community is insanely excited about the Internet. Internet companies are springing up like mushrooms, inspired by such amazing success stories as Amazon.com, which started doing business just a few years ago, and is already losing hundreds of millions of dollars a year. A LOT of Internet companies are losing money like crazy, yet their stock prices are soaring; in fact, the more an Internet company loses, the more desirable it becomes to investors. This seems like a paradox, but there's a very logical economic explanation: Internet investors have the brains of grapefruit. If you started a company called Set Fire to Piles of Money.com, they'd be beating down your door.

Here in the newspaper business, we have definitely caught Internet Fever. In the old days, we used to—get this!—actually *charge money* for our newspapers. Ha ha! What an old-fashioned, low-tech, non-digital concept! Nowadays all of the hip modern newspapers spend millions of dollars operating Web sites where we give away the entire newspaper for free. Sometimes we run advertisements in the regular newspaper urging our remaining paying customers to go to our Web sites instead. "Stop giving us money!" is the shrewd marketing thrust of these ads. Why do we do this? Because all the other newspapers are doing it! If all the other newspapers stuck pencils up their noses, we'd do that, too! This is called "market penetration."

My point is that if the newspaper industry—which still has not figured out, despite centuries of operation, where your driveway is—can get into the Internet, then you can, too. Simply follow the clear, detailed instructions set forth in this column, and you're on your way! I sincerely hope you get very, very rich. Because then I can be your friend.

This Real Man Can Drive Any Truck
Named Tonka

As a man, I believe that, every now and then, a man should do something manly. So when I got invited to the North Texas Earthmoving Field Day, my manly reaction was: "HECK yes."

The North Texas Earthmoving Field Day is a very manly annual event organized by the Texas Engineering Extension Service (TEEX), which is a member of the Texas A&M University System. The Earthmoving Field Day is a massive gathering of big studly machines of the type you sometimes see in the distance, pushing around humongous masculine piles of dirt. The basic idea behind Earthmoving Field Day is that people looking to buy heavy equipment can actually climb into the cabs of these machines and grab the controls and perform a "hands-on" assessment of their capabilities, by which I mean have a *whole* bunch of manly mechanized fun with those babies.

When I was maybe six years old, I spent many hours on a dirt pile next to my house, making roads and stuff with toy trucks and bulldozers. This was hard work, because in addition to pushing the heavy equipment around, I had to make the motor noise with my mouth—*BRRRMMMMMM*—for hours on end, keeping a fine mist of spit raining down on the construction site. Almost all boys do this, yet for some reason most of us, when we grow up, rarely operate any piece of equipment more impressive than hedge trimmers.

I flew to Dallas on an airplane full of hedge-trimmer-owning briefcase toters from the world of dot-com. But I entered a new realm entirely when I rented a car and drove west for a manly piece, into the country, until I saw a large testosterone cloud on the horizon, indicating the Earthmoving Field Day site. I joined a parade of pickup trucks headed for the top of a big old hill that was in danger of sinking under the weight of dozens and dozens of dozers, graders, loaders, trenchers, backhoes, cranes, scraper boxes, skid steers, rock crushers, and every other dang kind of machine that is designed to deliver, in no uncertain terms, the following message to the Earth: MOVE.

We're talking about some large units here. We're talking about machines the size of your house with wheels the size of your car, machines that get zero miles per gallon and have the word "WARNING" in big black letters all over them, followed by statements that inevitably begin, "TO PREVENT SERIOUS INJURY OR DEATH . . ."

Walking around, admiring and climbing into these rigs, were hundreds of guys, virtually every single one of whom wore work boots, Wrangler jeans, a T-shirt, and either a ball cap or a cowboy hat. Most wore belts with large manly buckles, some of which were pointing almost straight down under the weight of bellies large enough to contain Richard Simmons. These guys don't belong to health clubs: They chew tobacco while digging the holes that *become* health clubs.

I was given a tour of the Field Day by the guy who started it, Mike Griffith, a Texan who pronounces "vehicle" as "vee-hickle" and uses many Texas expressions such as "that vee-hickle is slick as a whistle." He gave me a ball cap and drove me around on a rugged vehicle that he preferred to drive directly through dirt mounds, rather than around them. Mike showed me various Field Day activities, which included safety seminars and skills competitions. But the main activity, which at any given moment hundreds of guys were engaged in, was randomly digging big holes and then filling them back in, or moving a mound of dirt the size of, say, Vermont, from one side of a field to another, and then moving it back. And if you don't think that would be fun, then you are, no offense, probably a woman.

I got to operate several pieces of equipment, including a great big yellow thing that is technically called an "excavator," although most of us would call it a "steam shovel." This thing could knock down a post office in 5 minutes, and—this is why I love America—they put it into the hands of a *humor columnist*. Onlookers ran for cover as, with my ball cap firmly on my head, I yanked randomly on the control levers, causing the giant metal shovel to zoom and flail around like a crazed robot dinosaur on speed. But I stayed with it, and finally I managed to pick up a huge wad of dirt, move it 25 feet, and drop it, slick as a whistle. In the old days, it would have taken a humor columnist *weeks* to do this.

Satisfied with my day's work, I went to the food tent and lined up with the other men for a manly meal of barbecued meat slabs with extra cholesterol brought in by truck. Then, sadly, it was time for me to return to the world of dot-com hedge trimmers. The only evidence of where I'd been was the dirt on my shoes. Also, there was some moisture on my rental-car dashboard. Because, driving back to the airport, I couldn't help making the motor noise.

Wrestling's First Rule: Cover Your "Masculine Region"

If there's one question that troubles every thinking person, it's this: Does cheating go on in professional wrestling?

In an effort to find an answer, I recently attended a tournament sanctioned by Florida Championship Wrestling. I chose FCW for two solid journalistic reasons:

- It is a venerable circuit in the "minor leagues" of professional wrestling, where the potential stars of tomorrow learn the ground rules, the "do's and don't's," that make up the ethical standards of the sport.
- It is near my house.

The FCW tournament I attended was held at the Miccosukee Indian Gaming Center, located west of Miami on the edge of the Everglades. This is one of the few gaming facilities where you can gamble on bingo, slot machines, poker, etc., and then—merely by walking a short distance—get eaten by alligators.

I watched the wrestling matches from a seat right next to the commissioner of FCW, Bernie Siegel. It is Commissioner Siegel's job to monitor the sport closely for cheating and impose stiff punishments on wrongdoers.

"I haven't had an eye exam in years," he told me.

In the first match, a wrestler who had been losing

suddenly gained the upper hand (so to speak) by kicking his opponent in a very sensitive masculine region.

"Did you see that?" I asked Commissioner Siegel.

"See what?" he answered.

The referee didn't see it either, even though he was standing about two feet from the wrestlers. It takes a special type of person to be a professional-wrestling referee, the type of person who, if he had been present when the *Hindenburg* was being consumed by a giant ball of flame, would have been looking, with intense interest, at the ground.

In the next match, a wrestler thumbed his opponent in the eye, yanked on his hair, and then choked him for approximately five minutes while the referee hovered alertly nearby, looking for violations.

"These are world-class athletes," observed Commissioner Siegel.

Next, in one of the featured matches, a wrestler named Larry Lane fought "Playboy" Bobby Davis, who is 350 pounds of highly disciplined, superbly trained, expertly conditioned fat. Lane was winning, but then Davis's "manager," a woman named Ebony, who was wearing a pair of shorts that would be two sizes too small for Barbie, distracted the referee while a third wrestler, Tony Apollo, who was supposed to be injured and who was not, technically, even in this match, climbed into the ring and whacked Lane over the head from behind with his crutch.

"I didn't see anything there," said Commissioner Siegel, before I even asked him.

In another featured match, a wrestler named Anthony "The South Beach Stud" Adonis distracted the referee by asking him about the rules ("Our referees are trained to be instructive at all times," said Commissioner

Siegel). For several minutes, while the referee patiently explained the rules, directly behind his back, Adonis's opponent, Billy Viper, was writhing on the mat in agony while being repeatedly kicked in the masculine region and clawed in the eyeball region by Adonis's manager, a woman named Babe.

"We've had people get their eyes gouged out," observed Commissioner Siegel, adding, "They become referees."

As he spoke, Tony Apollo, who was not technically in *this* match, either, slipped a folding chair into the ring for Anthony Adonis to whack Billy Viper with.

"It looks like he's slipping a chair into the ring," I said.

"I'll have to check the tape on that," said Commissioner Siegel.

In subsequent matches, a wrestler beat his opponent in the face with a cowbell (yes, a cowbell); a manager named Abudadein ("The Master of Darkness") used his staff ("The Staff of Darkness") to knock out a security guard; and Duke "The Dumpster" Droese appeared to be about to win his match when his opponent, the Cuban Assassin, clubbed him senseless with a flagpole holding a Cuban flag, which the Cuban Assassin's manager, a woman named Fantasy, had slipped into the ring unobserved.

"Is he allowed to hit him with the flagpole?" I asked.

"He hit him with the *flagpole*?" responded Commissioner Siegel.

All in all, it was an exciting evening of athletic competition. And although at times it appeared, to my untrained eye, that some of the contestants might possibly have been taking liberties with the rules of fair play, I realize that this could hardly be possible if the commissioner of Florida Championship Wrestling, who happens to be a licensed attorney and whose whole JOB is to keep an eye on things, did not see any violations. So rest easy, America: The popular sport of professional wrestling is definitely "on the up and up." Its integrity is protected by safeguards every bit as stringent as the ones used to protect America's most vital nuclear secrets. You think I'm joking.

You Don't Wanna Know What's Under His Hood

I may be 51 years old, but, darn it, I'm still a "rock-and-roll kind of animal." So when a friend named Gene offered me some tickets to a Beach Boys concert, I jumped at the chance. As a result, I strained my back and had to lie down for six days.

But after the pain subsided I was very excited, because I'm a huge Beach Boys fan. I'll never forget the first time I saw them in person, back in 1964, at a fantastic concert in New York . . . Wait, no, it was Philadelphia, and it might have been 1967. And come to think of it, it wasn't the Beach Boys; it was the Bee Gees. Or maybe the Turtles. It was definitely a plural name. Although now that I think of it, I'm not 100 percent sure I was there.

But never mind the details. The point is that I've loved the Beach Boys' music since *way-y-y* back when I was in junior high school, and America was happy and carefree because the Civil War was finally over. I went through puberty with the Beach Boys (not *literally,* of course; we all had separate rooms). Their songs expressed a new kind of feeling that was stirring deep within the bowels of my loins; a feeling of vulnerability, of tenderness, and—yes—of sexual desire.

For cars, I mean. When the Beach Boys sang "She's real fine, my 409 . . . my four-speed, dual-quad, Posi-Traction 409," they were giving voice to the fantasy

of every pimple-speckled male at Harold C. Crittenden Junior High. We *lusted* for Posi-Traction! Whatever
it was!

I still know all the words to all the Beach Boys' car
songs. When I'm driving, and the radio plays "Shut
Down," which is about a drag race, I sing along at the
top of my lungs: "He's hot with ram induction, but it's
understood; I got a fuel-injected engine sittin' under my
hood." The truth is that I have no idea what kind of
engine I have sittin' under my hood. I could have a food
processor sittin' under there. But the Beach Boys still
make me feel like Mr. Stud Piston.

And the Beach Boys were not just limited to car
songs. They took on the important social issues, too, in
songs such as "Be True to Your School" (actual lyric:
"Rah rah rah rah sis boom bah!") and "I Get Around"
(actual lyric: "I'm a real cool head! I'm makin' real good
bread!").

They don't make music like that these days. In fact,
sometimes they don't even make *music.* I saw a TV show
recently wherein a group of hip-hop DJs competed to see
who was the best at making sounds with a record turntable. They'd put the needle on a record, then they'd spin
the turntable forward and backward violently, thereby
creating unique, by which I mean ugly, noises. I used to
do that when I was seven, and my mom would yell,
"STOP FOOLING WITH THE RECORD PLAYER!"
But these guys were *serious;* they had expressions of
intense concentration, as though it took vast artistic skill
to simulate the sound of deranged squirrels fighting in
an amplifier. A panel of judges looked on, frowning
thoughtfully, as though they were listening to Beethoven's
Fifth Symphony (actual lyric: "Dum dum dum DUM").
I wanted to scream at the TV screen: "A turntable is

NOT A MUSICAL INSTRUMENT, you morons! It's an APPLIANCE, like a toaster-oven! Or an accordion!"

So, OK, I'm too old to appreciate hip-hop. But I'm smack dab in the middle of the Beach Boys' demographic, to judge from the crowd at the concert I attended. Many of us are grayer than we once were, and our loins are larger. But we still know how to "party hearty." We had our cell-phone ringers set on "vibrate" and were ready to ROCK AND ROLL when the Beach Boys stormed onto the stage.

OK, "stormed" is a little strong. "Shuffled" is more accurate. Because the Beach Boys have gotten older, too. Although some of them apparently have gotten *younger.* A couple of the ones I saw definitely had not been born when they made their first record.

But even though some of the older Beach Boys could enter the Ernest Hemingway Look-alike Contest, they still SOUND like the Beach Boys, and that was all that mattered. Within 15 minutes the crowd was on its feet (it would have been on its feet sooner, but it has to be careful with its back). The Beach Boys sang a medley of their car songs, and I sang right along with them, and when, together, we sang the technical part of "Little Deuce Coupe" ("She's ported and relieved, and she's stroked and bored") there was genuine emotion in my voice. But without question the highlight came when the entire crowd—not just us older folks in our 50s, but also the young people in their late 40s—joined together to sing "Barbara Ann," all of us united for the moment by our inability to remember that one verse that goes something like:

> *Tried Betty Sue*
> *Did the boogaloo*

Went to the zoo
And I saw a tiger poo

It was a great night. And even though I didn't get home until almost 10:20 p.m., I was so excited that I stayed awake until almost 10:27. 'Round, 'round, get around, I get around.

The Boob Tube

Recently, one of our local TV news shows in Miami did a special investigative report on—I swear—brassiere sizes. The station promoted this report relentlessly for several days. Every few minutes you'd hear an announcer's voice saying, with an urgency appropriate for imminent nuclear attack: "ARE YOU WEARING THE WRONG BRA SIZE??" You'd have thought that women were dropping dead in the street by the thousands as a result of improperly sized brassieres. I was becoming genuinely concerned about this problem, despite the fact that, except on very special occasions involving schnapps, I don't even *wear* a brassiere.

Unfortunately, although I saw dozens of promotions for this special investigative report, I never saw the report itself. I assumed that the message would be: "Wear the right size brassiere!" My editor, Tom Shroder, who has a keen interest in the issues, did watch the report, and he told me that it explored the troubling question of "women wearing brassieres that were tragically about 10 sizes too small for their breasts, which left said breasts with no other choice but to spill, tragically, out of the brassiere cups into the camera lens."

But my point here is not directly related to brassieres, although it IS a lot of fun to use the word "brassiere" in a newspaper column, brassiere brassiere brassiere. My point is that, pound for pound, the most dramatic and entertaining programming on television is your local TV news shows. Their only serious competition is the cable channel that, 24 hours a day, features the TV Evangelists With Hairdos The Size Of Adult Yaks.

If you don't receive the Big-Haired Evangelists channel, you need to march right down to your cable company and throw rocks through the windows until you get it, because these people are WAY more entertaining than any space alien you will ever see on *Star Trek*. My favorite is a woman with a gigantic mound of hair colored exactly the same designer shade as Bazooka brand bubble gum. Perhaps this fact explains why, almost every time I tune in, this woman is weeping. Her tear ducts must be as big as volleyballs. Using the standard evangelical measurement of Gallons of Weepage Per Broadcast (GWPB), this woman could very well be threatening the seemingly unbreakable records set back in the glorious '80s by Hall-of-Famer Tammy Faye Bakker. I would pay serious money to see a Weep-Off between these two great performers.

But as entertaining as these shows are, their message tends to be somewhat repetitive ("God loves you! So send us money!"). Whereas on your local TV news shows, they're always surprising you with dramatic new issues that you should be nervous about. Often these involve ordinary consumer items that, when subjected to the scrutiny of a TV news investigative report, mutate into deadly hazards. (John R. Gambling of radio station WOR in New York has a wonderful collection of promotions for these TV news reports, including one wherein the announcer says: *"TONIGHT AT SIX: YOUR DRY CLEANING CAN KILL YOU!!"*)

A while back, one of our Miami TV news shows—I think it was different from the one that warned us about improperly fitted brassieres brassieres brassieres—did a dramatic, heavily promoted investigative report on: frozen yogurt. This report, which seemed at least as long as *Alien Resurrection,* but scarier, investigated the possibility of deadly bacteria in our frozen-yogurt supply. If I understood the report correctly, there have never been any cases of any actual person actually being harmed by local frozen yogurt, but that seemed like a minor technicality. The point was: IT COULD HAPPEN! THE YOGURT OF DEATH!!

The way I have dealt with this menace is by taking the medical precaution of never eating frozen yogurt without first putting large quantities of chocolate fudge on it, on the scientific theory that the bacteria will eat the fudge and become too fat to do anything inside my body except sit around and belch. But I would not know to do this if it were not for local TV news.

I also would not know how I am supposed to feel about many stories if not for the fact that the TV news personalities make sad faces for sad stories and happy faces for happy stories. Sometimes, to make sure I understand the point, they come right out and tell me, at the end of each story, whether it was "tragic" or "nice."

FIRST PERSONALITY: What a tragic story, Bob.

SECOND PERSONALITY: Uh . . . no, it wasn't.

FIRST PERSONALITY: It wasn't?

SECOND PERSONALITY: No. That was the story about dogs playing mah-jongg.

FIRST PERSONALITY: Whoops! I had it confused with the story about the plane crashing into the orphanage! Ha ha!

SECOND PERSONALITY: Ha ha! Coming up, we'll have part four of our special investigative report: "Formica: Silent Killer In Your Kitchen."

Well, I see we've run out of time, so that's all for this week's column. Remember to be nervous about everything. And now for these words: brassiere brassiere brassiere.

And Don't Forget...
Tassels for All the Generals

Whatever you are doing, drop it right now, unless it is a baby. Because I have obtained some shocking information regarding our National Security—information that I am going to reveal to you now, despite the chilling fact that, by revealing it, I am placing myself in direct, personal peril of winning a Pulitzer Prize.

This information concerns some alarming military

research currently being conducted by a foreign power that represents the greatest single security threat to the United States, as measured not only by the magnitude of the physical danger, but also by the number of Celine Dion records.

That's right: I am referring to Canada. As you may recall, last year I urged the United States to declare war on Canada over the issue of toilet smuggling. In the United States, we have a federal law, enacted by Congress, requiring that new consumer toilets be limited to 1.6 gallons of water per flush. There is an excellent reason for this law: Congress has the brains of an eggplant. But that does not change the fact that it is a law.

Canada, however, flagrantly disobeys this law, on the grounds that—get THIS for a legal technicality—it is a foreign country. In Canada, anybody, including convicted felons and underage children, can walk into any toilet store, purchase a 3.5-gallon-per-flush toilet, and openly flaunt it on the street, and the authorities do NOTHING. As I reported, some of these toilets are finding their way across the border into the United States. And what is our government doing? It is shooting cruise missiles at the Balkans, which do not even HAVE toilets.

When are we, as a nation, going to wake up and recognize the REAL threat to our security? No doubt you are aware that just recently, in our nation's capital (Washington, D.C.), a number of highly strategic cherry trees were deliberately chewed by saboteur beavers. Ask yourself this: *Where do beavers come from?* The Balkans? No! Beavers come from Canada, and they take their orders from Canada and nobody else, as you know if you have ever tried to get one to fetch a ball.

And now, as if we did not already have enough reasons to declare war on Canada, comes word of this chilling research being conducted by the Canadian military.

I have here a news article from the Canadian Press, written by Dennis Bueckert and sent to me, at great personal risk, by an alert secret undercover agent in Canada named Lauren Leighton, M.D. This article, about a new Canadian armed-forces program, contains the following chilling sentence, which I swear I am not making up:

"An elite unit at National Defence headquarters is actively studying whether to proceed with development of the world's first combat bra."

You read that correctly: The Canadian military is working on *a combat brassiere*. The article quotes Captain Frank Delanghe, an officer with the $184 million Clothe the Soldier Program, as saying: "No army that I know of has ever touched or even approached this issue."

How can we, the American public, remain sanguine in the face of this news? Especially when we do not really know what "sanguine" means? How can we sit back and do nothing when an increasingly hostile, beaver-infested, big-toilet nation spends $184 million (nearly $37.50 American) on a program to develop a high-tech futuristic assault undergarment? How would you feel if you were an American soldier guarding our northern border, equipped with only a conventional brassiere—the basic design of which has not changed significantly since the Korean Conflict—knowing that at any moment, elite Canadian troops could come charging across No Person's Land toward you, and the first sight you would see—a sight that would strike terror into the heart of even the most hardened combat veteran—would be the Cones of Doom?

And while we are asking the tough questions, I have one here that was sent in by concerned reader Margaret Wilson of Santa Barbara, California, who wants to know:

How come we say "a pair of pants" and "a pair of shorts," but NOT "a pair of bras"?

I wish I could inform you that our so-called "Defense Department" was trying to answer these questions, but I cannot. And that is why I am urging you to write your congressperson NOW and tell him or her that you want the United States to launch a massive wasteful federal program to match Canada's military-undergarment research. Please keep your letter dignified. Do NOT lower yourself to cheesy wordplay such as "support our troops," or "stay abreast of our enemies," or "check out the Balkans on that lieutenant." If we can get Congress to approve such a program, I have no doubt that the president will take a personal interest, especially when he realizes that, once we have perfected the Tactical Field Brassiere, we could adapt the same technology for even more advanced weapons. I am referring, of course, to the Stealth Thong.

A Watchdog Never Drops His Guard—
Except for Dessert

Today's topic is: Home Security

Recently my wife and I went to the home of some friends for a dinner party involving three couples and numerous pets. Our hosts are fond of animals: They have a big herd of turtles living in a decorative pond outside, and three dogs patrolling inside. Actually, one of the dogs is only slightly more mobile than a shrub; he's around 47,000 years old in dog years and totally blind. He may in fact be medically dead. But dogs don't get all mopey over physical disabilities. This particular dog still maintains a productive routine, which consists of every now and then getting to his feet (this takes about an hour) and wandering around until he bumps into something, which he sniffs. If he thinks it might be food, he tries to eat it; if it bites back, he knows it's one of the other dogs.

The two younger dogs are more active; their job is to wait for people to come to the door, then bark loudly and angrily to communicate the fact that, based on their extensive experience as dogs, the people at the door are bad and somebody should bite them. Dogs are deeply suspicious of anybody using a door. Even if, when the door is opened, it turns out that the people standing there know the dogs, and in fact live in the house, the dogs will sometimes continue barking at them for a few seconds, in case it's some kind of trick.

Dogs behave this way because they are extremely vigilant (I am using "vigilant" in the sense of "stupid"). I have some friends named Libby and Buzz who have a small, nervous dog named Elmo who is so vigilant that he would be classified, on the scale of animal intelligence, in the category of "mineral." Elmo and Buzz have lived in the same house for several years now, but every time Buzz walks into a room where Elmo is on duty, Elmo reacts as though Buzz is an entire urban street gang, barking, growling, and running around in small, alarmed circles to let Libby know that Buzz is bad and she should bite him (she rarely does). After maybe 15 minutes, Elmo starts to remember who Buzz is, and he calms down. But if Buzz leaves the room for, say, 10 seconds, all the current drains out of Elmo's mental battery, and when Buzz returns, YIKES! RED ALERT! Elmo goes off again, like a small, furry, defective car alarm. It is not a quiet household. But by gosh it is a *secure* household, thanks to Elmo's vigilance.

But getting back to my story: We were having a nice dinner in our friends' home, and during this dinner one of the dogs kept going to a window and growling. We paid no attention, because dogs are always growling— maybe at the moon, maybe at the turtles, maybe at the Federal Reserve Board—who can say?

After dinner, all of us, including the dogs, went into another room to have dessert and watch the Miami Heat play an important basketball game. Actually, the women watched the game; the men actively controlled the outcome by shouting at the screen. The dogs watched the dessert.

Through skillful team shouting, we men won the

game, and everybody agreed it had been a pleasant evening. Then the women discovered that their purses, which had been in the kitchen, were gone. While we'd been shouting at the TV, a burglar had sneaked in and stolen them. He'd obviously been watching us through the window. The growling dog had been telling us this.

When we discovered the burglary, different people reacted in different ways. Some called the police; others smoked cigarettes, even though they have technically quit. I decided to go outside and look around the yard for Clues. Perhaps I would even find the perpetrator! Then, drawing on my prowess in the martial arts, I would wet my pants.

I was called back into the house by my wife, who had been informed by the police dispatcher that, by wandering around out in the dark, I was being really, really vigilant. The police came quickly. Needless to say, the dogs barked at them. (The young dogs, I mean; the dead dog merely checked to see if they were food.) We later concluded that the reason the dogs did NOT bark at the burglar was that (a) they were busy watching the dessert, and (b) the burglar came in through the window, which apparently is not a violation of dog security rules.

The next day the purses were found a few miles away, minus cash but still containing credit cards, drivers' licenses, makeup, tissues, pharmaceuticals, espresso machines, power tools and whatever else women keep in their purses. So it could have been a lot worse. And we can all learn some valuable lessons from this episode about home security, namely:

1. We should lock our doors AND windows.
2. Dogs will give you a lot of "false alarms," but every now and then they may really know what they're barking about.

3. On the other hand, maybe not.
4. Experts agree that, if you want REAL home security and peace of mind, turtles are worthless.

Nuke the Stalker Sparrow
That Fowled Fabio

Before I get to today's topic, which is celebrity-attacking birds, I want to issue a formal apology to the "Tri Cities."

The "Tri Cities" are Pasco, Richland, and Kennewick, Washington, which call themselves the "Tri Cities" in proud recognition of the fact that there are three of them. I had not heard of these cities until recently, when I wrote a column about the Hanford contaminated nuclear dump site, which is located near the "Tri Cities." My column was about the fact that radioactive ants, flies, and gnats had been discovered at Hanford; I expressed concern that they might mutate and become gigantic and attack Los Angeles and suck all the blood out of actress Fran Drescher.

This column prompted a somewhat critical article in *The Tri-City Herald,* which is the leading newspaper in the "Tri Cities" area. The article pointed out that my column, in focusing on radioactive insects, ignored many of the positive things happening in the "Tri Cities" area, such as (these are direct quotes) "the winning Tri-City Americans hockey team" and "the booming construction going on behind Columbia Center mall."

The Tri-City Herald article prompted yet ANOTHER article, this one in *The Seattle Times* (motto: "We Cover *The Tri-City Herald*"). The *Times* article quoted a "communications specialist" with the Hanford cleanup company who objected to my statement that the dump site "glows like a Budweiser sign." The communications specialist states: "That's a little bit more than inaccurate."

The *Times* story also notes that:

- Authorities prefer to call the insects "contaminated," rather than "radioactive."
- According to the president of The Tri-City Visitors and Convention Bureau (this is another direct quote): "The reality is that the real story, so to speak, is that the community has many positive attributes, like a great quality of life."
- The Hanford site also produces (I swear I am not making this up) contaminated tumbleweeds "on a regular basis."

So anyway, I feel terrible. The first rule of journalistic balance is: "Before you report that an area has radioactive ants, ALWAYS check to see if it also has a winning minor-league hockey team." And I violated that rule. So I hereby apologize to the "Tri Cities." I'm sure it's a wonderful area that everybody should visit immediately. To help promote tourism there, I've come up with some slogans:

- "The Tri Cities Area . . . Contaminated—NOT Radioactive!"
- "Relax! That Booming Sound You Hear Is Nothing More Than Construction Behind the Columbia Center Mall!"

There! I hope that patches things up between me and the "Tri Cities." If there is anything else that I, personally, can do from 3,000 miles away, please let me know!

Now let's turn to celebrity-attacking birds. I broach

this topic in light of an alarming recent incident involving Fabio, the megahunk male supermodel with long flowing hair and a certain special way of looking at a woman that says to her: "My chest is the size of a UPS truck."

On March 30, Fabio was at the Busch Gardens theme park in Williamsburg, Virginia, to help inaugurate a new roller-coaster ride, "Apollo's Chariot," named for Apollo, the ancient Roman god of motion sickness. With the press on hand to witness this historic event, Fabio climbed into a seat in the front row of the coaster, and off he went. At some fateful point during the two-minute ride, Fabio collided with—you guessed it—a contaminated tumbleweed.

No, seriously, he collided with a bird. He was not seriously hurt, but in the Associated Press photo I saw, he had blood on his nose and the stunned look of a man who has gone beak-to-beak with Terror.

Busch Gardens officials attempted to downplay the incident, calling it "relatively minor." They told the press that nearly a million people have ridden roller coasters there, and Fabio was the first one ever to collide with a bird. We do not have to be trained statisticians to understand what this means: It means *the bird did it on purpose.* The bird community has probably been waiting for *years* to get Fabio up in a roller coaster and take a whack at him.

And this will not be the end of it. As any bird scientist (or "orthodontist") will tell you: Once a bird tastes celebrity blood, it wants more. Today it is Fabio; tomorrow it could be the Spice Girls. That's why I urge President Clinton to go on TV and bite his lip in a sincerely weepy manner until Congress approves a program wherein we lash expendable volunteer celebrities such as Dennis Rodman, The McLaughlin Group, and actress

Fran Drescher to roller coasters and send them up around the clock until they are attacked by birds, at which point F-16 fighter escorts open fire (on the birds).

Let's do this NOW. Let's not wait until celebrity roller-coaster attack birds—which, like "contaminated tumbleweeds," would be an excellent name for a rock band—puncture a truly irreplaceable national treasure such as, God forbid, Adam Sandler. Let's keep our nation free from terror, from sea to glowing sea.

Batman to the Rescue

One evening my wife mentioned, casually, that she had been talking to the son of one of her friends, a little boy named Alexander, about his upcoming fourth birthday.

"Alexander says he's having a Batman party," my wife said.

"Hm," I said.

"So I told him that maybe Batman would come to the party," my wife said.

"Hm," I said.

My wife said nothing then. She just looked at me. Suddenly, I knew who was going to be Batman.

I was not totally opposed. In my youth I read many Batman comics, and it seemed to me that he had a pretty neat life, disguised as wealthy playboy Bruce Wayne, waiting for the police commissioner of Gotham City to shine the Bat Signal onto the clouds (it was always a cloudy night when the commissioner needed Batman). Then Bruce would change instantly—it took him only one comic-book panel—into his Batman costume and roar off in the Batmobile to do battle with the Forces of Evil or attend a birthday party.

Of course Bruce owned his own Batman costume. I had to rent mine. It consisted of numerous black rubber pieces, similar to automobile floor mats, with strings so you could tie them to your body. One piece was shaped like rippling chest muscles, so you could transform your-self, like magic, from a flabby weakling into a flabby weak-ling wearing an automobile floor mat.

It took me a lot longer than one comic panel to get into this costume, but finally I was ready to speak the words that strike fear into the hearts of criminals every-where: "Michelle, could you tie my G-string?" It turns out that a key part of the Batman costume is this trian-gular floor mat piece that protects the Bat Region. It's very difficult to attach this piece to yourself without help, which could explain why Batman hooked up with Robin.

At last I was ready. In full Bat regalia, I stepped out of the house, and—as crazy as this may sound—for the first time I truly understood, as only a crusader for jus-tice can understand, why people do not wear heavy black rubber outfits in South Florida in August. Stag-gering through the armor-piercing sunshine and 384 per-cent humidity, I made it to the Batmobile, which was disguised as a wealthy playboy's Toyota Celica.

When we got to Alexander's house, in accordance with our Bat Plan, I remained outside in the Batmobile while Michelle went to the backyard, where the party was going on. We had bought Alexander a Batman walkie-talkie set; Michelle gave Alexander one unit and told him to use it to call Batman. These Batman walkie-talkies con-tain actual transistors, so when Alexander called me, I was able to hear, on the other unit, clear as a bell, a ran-dom bunch of static. Interpreting this as the Bat Signal, I pulled the rubber Bat Cowl over my head, thus render-ing myself legally blind, and drove the Toyota Batmobile into the backyard.

The effect on the party guests, as you would expect, was electrifying. The adults were so electrified that some of them almost wet themselves. The younger guests were stunned into silence, except for Matthew, age one, who ran, crying, to his mom, and probably did wet himself.

With all eyes upon me, I stopped the Batmobile, flung the door open, and, in one fluid, manly motion, sprang out of the seat, then got retracted violently back into the seat, because I had forgotten to unfasten my seat belt. Eventually I was able to disentangle my cape and stride in a manly, rubberized way over to the birthday boy.

"Happy birthday, Alexander!" I said, using a deep Bat Voice. After that the conversation lagged, because, let's be honest, what are you going to talk to Batman about? The pennant races? So we just stood there for a while, with Alexander staring at me, and me trying to look manly and calm despite the fact that after 30 seconds in the sun I could have fried an egg on top of my cowl.

Finally the cake arrived, and everybody sang "Happy Birthday," and I announced that I had to go fight crime. Striding back to the Batmobile, I opened the car door, turned dramatically toward the youngsters, and said, quote "BWEEPBWEEPBWEEPBWEEP." Actually, it was the Batmobile that said this, because I had forgotten to deactivate the Bat Alarm. I climbed into the front seat, slammed the door with several inches of cape sticking out the bottom, and backed manfully and blindly into the street. Fortunately there was nothing in my way, because I would definitely have hit it, and the law would not have been on my side. ("Mr. Barry, please tell the jury exactly what you were wearing as you backed your car over the plaintiff.")

The next day, Alexander's mom reported that the first thing he did when he woke up was turn on his walkie-talkie and call Batman. He said he could hear Batman, but Batman couldn't hear him because he was busy fighting evil supercriminals named Poison Ivy and Mr. Freeze.

This was almost true: Batman was actually battling Heat Rash. So he will be out of action for a while. The next superhero from this household to visit Alexander—and I have made this very clear to Michelle—will definitely be Cat Woman.

The Fountain of Youth

Recently I was at a party hosted by a younger couple, defined as "a couple that had not yet been born when I started worrying about cholesterol." You will never guess whose music these young people were playing: Bobby Darin's. Yes. Bobby Darin, hepcat swinger from my youth, is cool again!

No doubt you've read about how the Hot New Trend among "with-it" 20-something people is to eschew the rock scene and pretend that they're swank sophisticates living three or four decades ago—drinking martinis, going to nightclubs, dressing like the late Frank Sinatra (not the women, of course; they're dressing like the late Dean Martin), voting for Dwight Eisenhower, using words like "eschew," etc. This makes me wonder: If old things are cool, could *I* become cool again?

I have not felt remotely cool for a long time, thanks largely to the relentless efforts of my teenage son, whose goal in life is to make me feel 3,500 years old. We'll be in the car, and he'll say, "You wanna hear my new CD?" And I, flattered that he thinks his old man might like the same music he does, will say "Sure!" So he increases the sound-system volume setting from "4" to "Meteor Impact," and he puts in a CD by a band with a name like "Pustule," and the next thing I know gigantic nuclear bass notes have blown out the car windows and activated both the driver- and passenger-side air bags, and I'm writhing on the floor, screaming for mercy with jets of blood spurting three feet from my ears. My son then ejects the CD, smiling contentedly, knowing he has purchased a winner. On those extremely rare occasions when I *like* one of his CDs, I imagine he destroys it with a blowtorch.

My point is that, for some time, I have viewed myself as being roughly equal, on the Coolness Scale, to Bob Dole. And then, suddenly, at this party, these 20-somethings were playing Bobby Darin, a singer from my youth, an era known as "The Era When There Were a Lot of Singers Named Bobby and One Named Freddy" (Bobby Sherman, Bobby Vee, Bobby Vinton, Bobby Rydell, Elvis "Bobby" Presley, and Freddy "Boom Boom" Cannon).

I KNOW Bobby Darin's music. Whenever I hear his swinging version of "(Oh My Darlin') Clementine" I snap my fingers in a happening "jive" manner and sing right along with these immortal lyrics:

> *You know she would rouse up*
> *Wake all of them cows up*

(They don't write them like that anymore. They can't: They have been medicated.)

I vividly remember when Bobby Darin had a hit record with "Mack the Knife," which is sometimes referred to as "The Sgt. Pepper's Lonely Hearts Club Band of 1959," because it was nearly three minutes long and had weird incomprehensible lyrics involving somebody named "Sukey Tawdry." I remember going to a record hop— that's right, an actual *record hop*—in the gymnasium of Harold C. Crittenden Junior High in Armonk, New York, where they played "Mack the Knife" maybe 14 times and we all danced the Jitterbug.

The Jitterbug was a dance wherein you remained in actual, physical contact with your partner—what kids now call "touch-dancing." I grew up at the tail end of the touch-dancing era; after that, we started doing non-touch dances—the Jerk, the Boogaloo, the Cosine, the Funky Downtown Rutabaga, etc., wherein you strayed several feet from your partner. Later in the '60s, songs got longer and dance standards got looser, and you often lost visual contact altogether with your partner, sometimes winding up, days later, in completely different states. This was followed by the disco era, during which you and your partner might touch briefly, but only for the purpose of exchanging narcotics; which in turn was followed by the "mosh pit" concept of dancing, wherein you dance simultaneously with many people, the object being to inflict head injuries on them.

So for decades, the only time you saw touch-dancing was at wedding receptions, when the band—as required by federal wedding-reception law—played "Bad, Bad Leroy Brown," and guests age 73 and older would hobble onto the floor and do the Fox Trot while younger people gyrated randomly around them.

But now touch-dancing is back, and I'm excited about it, because—ask anybody who has seen me at a wedding reception after the bar opens—I can still do the Jitterbug. I can get out there on the floor and really whirl my partner around. Granted, sometimes my partner winds up face-down in the wedding cake, but that is not the point. The point is that, despite what my son thinks, *maybe I am cool again.* I'm thinking about putting a tube and a half of Brylcreem in my hair and going to a swank nightclub. I'd saunter up to the bar, order a dry martini, and settle back to soak up the scene; then, when a really "swinging" song came on, I'd get to my feet and "wow" the younger generation when I, in a suave and sophisticated manner, threw up on my shoes, because martinis make me sick.

Then I'd go to bed, because I'm 3,500 years old.

He Would Flee Bosoms, But His Car Is Booted

Vacation season is approaching, so today I want to issue a Travel Warning to help you avoid a menace that could completely ruin your vacation: bosoms.

This menace was brought to my attention by a recent letter to my newspaper, *The Miami Herald* (motto: "Keep Looking! It's Somewhere in Your Yard!"). This letter was written by the Reverend Keith A. Marvel of Wilmington, Delaware. He states:

> Three friends and I recently visited Miami to get in a little Florida sunshine and some golf. Our four-day stay was a bit of a shock.
>
> First we thought maybe we landed in another country when we walked to a beach—marked for our hotel's guests only—only to find topless women sunbathers.
>
> As Christian men, we are taught to flee this type of thing, which is hard in Miami since it seemed that this type of immorality was nearly everywhere.
>
> Then, the clincher came at 7 P.M. Saturday night when we went to get dinner and came back to find our car, which was "booted" by a company.

After describing his group's unsuccessful efforts to protest the $25 parking fine, the Reverend Marvel states:

239

"I hope that the city of Miami Beach would do something about this ordinance and topless sunbathing. If not, maybe you should warn tourists before they spend their hard-earned money on a trip to Miami."

First, by way of sincere apology, let me state, on behalf of all of the citizens of Miami and Miami Beach, who have unanimously elected me to speak for them, that the letters in "Keith A. Marvel" can be rearranged to spell "Hark! Evil Meat!"

Let me also state that the Reverend Marvel is correct: There are topless women sunbathers in Miami, although I think it's a stretch to say they're "nearly everywhere." I've lived in Miami for 13 years, and if it were infested with topless women, I definitely would have noticed. Also it would be mentioned on the TV news.

ANNOUNCER: What's our forecast, Bob?
WEATHERPERSON: Bill, I look for warmer temperatures and continued naked bosoms all over the place, so the public should remain indoors with duct tape over its eyes.

It's not as bad as that. But we do get our topless sunbathers. Most of them are tourists from Europe, which is known for being immoral. Europeans openly smoke cigarettes; they think nothing of toplessness. You cannot turn around in Europe without seeing a marble statue of a topless ancient Greek or Roman goddess the size of a Budweiser Clydesdale, expressing the ancient artistic concept: "I cannot find a marble brassiere in my size."

So European women often sunbathe topless. European men are also quite exposed. Apparently there was some huge mixup over in Europe, whereby all the eye patches were mislabeled as men's bathing suits, the result being that European men at the beach often have nothing covering their Euros but a piece of fabric the size of a Cheez-It. Meanwhile, Europeans who injure their eyes are stumbling around with swimming trunks over their heads.

On my fact-finding trips to Miami-area beaches, I've noticed that the Europeans don't seem to notice that they're almost naked. But the Americans definitely do. American women are cool about it; they have developed the ability to look at things, such as a man's Euro region, via a Stealth Glance technique, so that you never actually catch them doing it. (They use a similar technique for scratching.) American men, on the other hand, are as subtle as a dog with its nose in another dog's butt. When an American man catches sight of a bosom, his head snaps toward it, his eyeballs lock onto it like missile radar, and a loud alarm goes off in his brain, similar to the one in submarine movies that goes "DIVE! DIVE! DIVE!"—except it goes "BOSOM! BOSOM! BOSOM!" As long as the man is within range of the bosom (12 miles) his head will remain pointed toward it and he will be unable to think about anything else; this is the primary cause of freighters running aground.

The point is that if a man, for example the Reverend Marvel, is on the same beach as a bosom, he is physiologically incapable of simply ignoring it. He has to look! And then of course he has to flee. This is why I am issuing the following warning to travelers: IF YOU COME TO THE MIAMI AREA, AND YOU GO TO THE BEACH, THERE IS A CHANCE YOU WILL SEE TOPLESS SUNBATHERS. The Miami tourist bureau requests that you tell everybody you know about this warning and spread it on the Internet. The Orlando tourist bureau has also asked me to warn you that they have a bosom problem there, but the Miami bureau claims that most of the Orlando ones are artificial.

Let me conclude by thanking the Reverend Marvel for alerting the world to this danger. As a token of our appreciation, we will have the people who booted his car executed without trial. And we will make every effort to rid our community of decadent, hedonistic, and degenerate activities. We'll start with golf.

The Birth of Wail

When I heard that Richard Berry, the man who wrote "Louie Louie," had died, I said . . .

Well, I can't tell you, in a family newspaper, what I said. But it was not a happy remark. It was the remark of a person who realizes he'll never get to thank somebody for something.

I remember the day I first heard "Louie Louie." I was outside my house, playing basketball with my friends on a "court" that featured a backboard nailed to a tree next to a geologically challenging surface of dirt and random rocks, which meant that whenever anybody dribbled the ball, it would ricochet off into the woods and down the hill, which meant that our games mostly consisted of arguing about who would go get it.

So we spent a lot of our basketball time listening to a transistor radio perched on a tree stump, tuned to WABC in New York City. (I mean the radio was tuned to WABC; the stump was tuned to WOR.) And one miraculous day in 1963, out of the crappy little transistor speaker came . . .

Well, you know what it sounds like: This guy just *wailing* away, totally unintelligibly, with this band just *whomping* away behind him in the now-legendary "Louie" rhythm, whomp-whomp-whomp, whomp-whomp, whomp-whomp-whomp . . .

And it was just SO cool. It was 500 million times cooler than, for example, Bobby Rydell. It was so cool that I wanted to dance to it right there on the rocky dirt court, although of course as a 15-year-old boy of that era I would have sawed off both my feet with a nail file before I would have danced in front of my friends.

I loved "Louie Louie" even before I found out that it had dirty words. Actually, it turned out that it *didn't* have dirty words, but for years we—and when I say "we," I am referring to the teenagers of that era, and J. Edgar Hoover—were all convinced that it did, which of course just made it cooler. We loved that song with no idea whatsoever what it was about.

But for me the coolest thing about "Louie Louie" was this: I could play it on the guitar. In fact, just about *anybody* could play it, including a reasonably trainable chicken. Three chords, nothing tricky. This is why, when I—like so many teenage boys of that era—became part of a band in a futile attempt to appeal to girls, "Louie Louie" was the first song we learned. We'd whomp away on our cheap, untunable guitars plugged into our Distort-O-Matic amplifiers, and our dogs would hide and our moms would leave the house on unnecessary errands, and we'd wail unintelligibly into our fast-food-drive-thru-intercom-quality public-address system, and when we were finally done playing and the last out-of-tune notes had leaked out of the room, we'd look at each other and say, "Hey! We sound like the Kingsmen!" And the beauty of that song is, we kind of *did*.

I continued playing in bands in college, and many other songs went into and out of our repertoire, but we always played "Louie Louie." Over the years, musical and cultural critics have offered countless explanations for the song's enduring appeal, but I would say, based on playing it hundreds of times in front of a wide range of audiences, that the key musical factor is this: Drunk people really like it. My band found that, if large beer-guzzling college-fraternity members became boisterous and decided they wanted to play our instruments, or hit us, or hit us with our instruments, all we had to do was play "Louie Louie," and they would be inspired to go back to dancing and throwing up on their dates.

Sometimes people got a little TOO inspired. One night we were playing in a frat house at the University of Pennsylvania, and during "Louie Louie," an entire sofa—a *large* sofa—came through the front window, which was not open at the time. The crowd did not stop dancing, and we did not stop playing; we kept right on wailing and whomping. That's the kind of indestructible song "Louie Louie" is. I'm confident that it's one of the very few songs that would be able to survive a global thermonuclear war (another one is "Wild Thing").

I'm not defending it as art. I'm not saying that, as a cultural achievement, it is on a par with the *Mona Lisa,* or *Hamlet.* On the other hand, when the *Mona Lisa* or *Hamlet* comes on my car radio, I do not crank the volume way up and wail unintelligibly at my windshield. I still do this for "Louie Louie."

And for that, Richard Berry, wherever you are: Thanks.

Survival of Mankind Rides on the
Successful Pickup Line

So I was at this party, and I wound up at a table where three attractive single women were complaining about— Surprise!—men. Specifically, they were complaining about the pickup lines that had been used on them in a bar a few nights earlier.

One woman said: "This guy comes up to me and says, 'Are you a teacher?' I mean, is that supposed to be *romantic*?"

All three women rolled all six of their eyes.

Another one of them said: "This guy says to me, 'I've been looking at you all night!' So I go, 'Hel-LO, we just GOT here.'"

At this point all three women—and I want to stress that these are intelligent, nice women—were laughing. Not me. I was feeling bad for the guys.

I realize that there are certain hardships that only females must endure, such as childbirth, waiting in lines for public-restroom stalls, and a crippling, psychotic obsession with shoe color. Also, females tend to reach emotional maturity very quickly, so that by age seven they are no longer capable of seeing the humor in loud inadvertent public blasts of flatulence, whereas males can continue to derive vast enjoyment from this well into their 80s.

So I grant that it is not easy being a female. But I contend that nature has given males the heaviest burden of all: the burden of always having to Make the First Move, and thereby risk getting Shot Down. I don't know WHY males get stuck with this burden, but it's true throughout the animal kingdom. If you watch the nature shows on the Discovery Channel, you'll note that whatever species they are talking about—birds, crabs, spiders, clams—it is ALWAYS the male who has to take the initiative. It's always the male bird who does the courting dance, making a total moron of himself, while the female bird just stands there, looking aloof, thinking about what she's going to tell her girlfriends. ("And then he hopped around on one foot! Like I'm supposed to be impressed by THAT!")

Male insects have it the worst. The Discovery Channel announcer is always saying things like: "After the mating, the female mantis bites off the male mantis's head, and then she and her girlfriend mantises use it to play a game that looks a lot like Skee Ball."

Because I live in Florida, my patio is basically a giant singles bar for lizards. On any given day during mating season, I'll see dozens of male lizards out there making their most suave lizard move, which consists of inflating and deflating a red pouch under their chins. They seem to think that female lizards really go for a guy with a big chin pouch, but I have never once, in 14 years of close observation, seen a female respond. They just squat there looking bored, while all around them males are blinking on and off like defective warning lights.

Every now and then you'll see an offbeat TV news story about some animal, usually a moose, that has for some reason fallen in love with, and decided to relentlessly court, something totally inappropriate, such as a lawn tractor. This animal is ALWAYS a male. On the TV, they show it hanging around the lawn tractor with a big, sad, moony look, totally smitten, while the lawn tractor cruelly ignores it.

My point here is that, in matters of the heart, males have the brains of a walnut. No, wait! That is not my point. My point is that perhaps you women could cut us males a little bit of slack in the move-making process, because we are under a lot of stress. I vividly remember when I was in 10th grade, and I wanted to call a girl named Patty and ask her to a dance, and before I picked up the phone, I spent maybe 28 hours rehearsing exactly what I was going to say. So when I actually made the call, I was pretty smooth.

"Hello, Dance?" I said. "This is Patty. Do you want to go to the Dave with me?"

Fortunately Patty grasped the basic thrust of my gist and agreed to go to the dance. This was a good thing, because if she had shot me down, I would have been so humiliated that I would have never been able to go back to school. I would have dropped out of 10th grade and lied about my age and joined the U.S. armed forces, and as a direct result the Russians would have won the Cold War.

That is the awesome power that you women have over us men. I hope you understand this, and the next time a guy walks up and uses some incredibly lame, boneheaded line on you, I hope that, instead of laughing at him, you will remember that he is under the intense pressure of wanting to impress you enough so that you might want to get to know him better and maybe eventually, perhaps within the next 15 minutes, mate with him, thereby enabling the survival of the human race, which believe me is the only thing that we males are truly concerned about.

In conclusion, let me just say to all females everywhere, on behalf of all males everywhere, that you are very beautiful and your eyes are like two shining stars, unless you're a female fly, in which case your eyes are more like 2,038 shining stars. So please give us a chance. And if *you're* not interested, could you introduce us to your lawn tractor?

Baby Hormones Have Taken Over My Wife, and All I Can Say Is "Waaah!"

The most powerful force in the universe is not any kind of nuclear energy. It is not magnetism, gravity, or the IRS. The most powerful force in the universe is hormones. If you don't believe me, conduct the following simple scientific experiment:

1. Take a normal woman.
2. Get her pregnant.
3. See if she can walk past a display of baby shoes without stopping.

I've been conducting this experiment for several months now with my wife, Michelle. She's pregnant, and I have reason to believe that I'm the father. I'm excited about this, because I'm at an age—52—when many of my friends are thinking about retiring to dull, meaningless lives of travel, leisure, recreation, and culture. Not me! I'm about to start all over again with a brand-new little Miracle of Life to love, nurture, and—above all—become intimately familiar with the poops of.

But so far the big change in my life has been Michelle's behavior. She has never been a particularly maternal person; she's a professional sportswriter who has always been one of the guys. She understands the triangle offense and can watch football longer than I can. I've seen her fight her way through frenzied locker-room media mobs to get quotes from giant, sweaty football players. I've seen her stand on the field of 3Com Park in San Francisco right before a baseball play-off game, arguing in Spanish and not backing down one millimeter from a professional baseball player who was (1) VERY angry about something she had written and (2) holding a baseball bat.

Like many career women, Michelle insisted that becoming a mother would not change her. She was going to be the same professional person, darn it! She was NOT going to turn into one of those women who babble obsessively about the baby and baby clothes and all the other baby fixin's. Above all, she was NEVER going to drive a minivan.

Right.

I would estimate that, at the present time, my wife's blood supply is 92 percent baby-related hormones. Doctors often call hormones "the Saddam Husseins of the human body" because they are moody, and when they give commands, they expect instant obedience. So for now my wife is not my wife: She is the official spokesperson for crazed dictator hormones. When the hormones wake up, they do NOT want an affectionate "good morning" kiss. They want AN UNCOOKED POP-TART, and they want it RIGHT NOW. You do not question them, because they will throw up on you.

The hormones also want baby shoes. I don't know why. I have seen the baby, at the doctor's office, via a procedure called a "sonogram," and although, of course, I think it is a very beautiful and gifted child, it looks, more than anything, like a wad of gum. I frankly cannot imagine, given its current lifestyle in the womb, that footwear is a high priority.

But you try telling this to the hormones. They are

CRAZY for baby shoes. My wife could be fleeing from an armed robber, but if she ran past a display of baby shoes, her hormones would demand that she stop, pick up a shoe, and exclaim to whomever is nearby, even the robber, "Look how CUTE!" The smaller the shoe, the cuter the hormones think it is. If somebody came out with a baby shoe the size of a molecule, which could be viewed only through a very powerful microscope, my wife's hormones would make her buy 27 pairs.

The hormones also want baby outfits. Even though the baby is still deep inside my wife and would be very hard to dress without surgical instruments, it already has at least as many outfits as Elizabeth Taylor. If you come to our house for any reason, including to fix an appliance, the hormones will make my wife show you these outfits one at a time, and as each one is held up, you will be expected to agree that it is cute.

Lately, the hormones have become obsessed with the decor of the baby's room. They definitely wanted a Winnie the Pooh theme, but they spent weeks agonizing over whether to go with the Regular Pooh or the Classic Pooh theme. They finally decided on Classic Pooh, but, of course, now they must decide which of the estimated 14 million Classic Pooh baby-room accessories they will need. This is an important issue, and the hormones think about it all the time, even during football games. Any day now, Michelle is going to walk up to a defensive tackle in the Miami Dolphins locker room and ask him what he thinks about the Pooh ceiling border. This is not her fault. She is merely the vehicle: The hormones are driving.

Speaking of which, they want a minivan.

Today's Baby Showers Require an Ark to Haul Home the Loot

Whew! I am exhausted, physically and emotionally, and I will tell you why: I have been helping my wife register for her baby shower.

This is a new wrinkle in the field of having babies. When I was born, during the presidency of James K. Polk, we babies did not require a lot of equipment. We had our blanket, and that was pretty much it. We'd lie on our blanket and amuse ourselves for weeks on end by trying to get our feet into our mouths. If we were lucky, we'd have a rattle, which we would obtain by catching an actual rattlesnake with our tiny bare hands. Also in those days we changed our own diapers.

So back then, baby showers were pretty basic. There was no registering. A group of women would simply get together and watch as the mother-to-be opened the gifts and commented on them ("A blanket! Thank you! Look! Another blanket! That'll come in handy! Look! ANOTHER . . . ," etc.). In 20 minutes, the shower was over and everybody went back to pounding clothes with rocks.

Equipping your modern baby is a whole different kettle of fish. You've seen newsreels of the Normandy Invasion, with thousands of supply ships stretching across the English Channel as far as the eye can see? That will give you an idea of the minimum amount of things that you need to adequately support a single modern baby, in the view of today's baby industry.

So now, when you have a baby shower, you register what your baby-equipment needs are. We registered at a baby-fixin's megastore the size of Yellowstone National Park. The lady behind the counter handed us a sheet of paper that said "BABY REGISTRY MUST HAVES!" It listed MUST HAVE! baby items in seven categories: First Priorities, Room Decor, At Home, Splash Down, On The Go, Just For Fun, and Layette. (The baby industry says "Layette" because it sounds classier than "Clothes For Baby To Poop In.")

I added up all the items in the seven categories, and it came out to more than 150 things—furniture, bedding, undergarments, outergarments, warmers, coolers, bath gizmos, sterilizers, stabilizers, transporters, transponders, diaper anti-stink devices, a type of pump I don't even want to think about, and on and on—that the baby MUST HAVE! The piece of paper didn't say what would happen if you didn't get all of these things, but the clear implication is that your baby would fall behind all the other babies. Like, say you didn't get a jumper, which is a MUST HAVE! device that you put the baby in so it can bounce up and down while it is pooping. Without this device, your baby would be slower to develop the vital bouncing skills that studies have shown ultimately determine who gets into what business school.

And you can't just get any jumper. There are MANY jumpers, and you have to pick out the RIGHT one, the one that conforms to all 387 parts of the U.S. Department of Consumer Nervousness Jumper Safety Guidelines, because if you pick out the WRONG one, you could very well be signing your baby's death warrant. Multiply this responsibility by your 150 MUST HAVE!

items, and you begin to see the intense psychological pressures involved in registering for a baby shower.

The most stressful part is picking out the stroller. Today's baby stroller is an extremely high-tech piece of equipment, comparable in complexity to the B-1 bomber, but more expensive. I have purchased houses in less time than it took us to decide on a stroller. And I still agonize that we picked the wrong one. I mean, the stroller is not just a seat with wheels: It is a place where your baby will spend much of its critical developmental years pooping. You cannot afford to make a mistake.

The only good part of the shower-registration process was that I had a gun. I don't mean a bullet-shooting gun: I mean an electronic scanning gun, the kind that beeps when you point it at an item's Universal Product Code. This is how the baby megastore keeps track of what items you've registered for. All around the store, there were massively pregnant women, crazed by hormones, holding up tiny garments and going, "Awww! How CUTE!" And next to each woman was a man, finger on the trigger button of his scanning gun, ready to beep. It was like prehistoric times, when the woman's job was to bear the child, and the man's job was to hunt game and kill it by striking it with his club in the vulnerable product-code region.

So anyway, we registered for all kinds of stuff, which I guess means that once the shower is over, all that we'll be missing is the actual baby. Although, come to think of it, maybe we don't need the baby. It definitely was not on the MUST HAVES! list.

Labor Dispute

So my wife and I are preparing for childbirth. When I say "my wife and I," I, of course, mean "my wife." She will be the most directly involved.

On behalf of all men, I just want to take a moment here to get down on my knees and thank whoever invented our current biological system, under which the woman's job is to have the baby somehow go from the inside of her body to the outside of her body, in clear violation of every known law of physics, and the man's job is to stand around looking supportive and periodically, no matter what is actually happening to the woman, say, in an upbeat and perky voice, "You're doing great!"

My wife thinks the only fair system would be if, every time the woman had a contraction, she got to hit her husband on the body part of her choice with a ball-peen hammer. Of course, she is kidding. But only because her contractions have not yet started.

We've been going to childbirth classes, which involve sitting in a classroom filled with expectant couples and a mounting sense of dread. The teacher usually starts with a scientific discussion of childbirth, in which she shows us various diagrams and models to give us an idea of what will be happening when the Big Moment arrives. In my opinion, the most informative way to do this would be to hold up a bowling ball and a drinking straw, and say:

"Basically, THIS has to go through THIS. Ha ha!"

But our teacher keeps it fairly technical. After a while, we're starting to feel confident about this childbirth thing. We're thinking, "OK, all that has to happen is the cervix has to dilate to 10 centimeters! How hard can that be? I wonder what a cervix is? Also, what's a centimeter?"

So we're pondering these abstract questions and maybe thinking about what we're going to have for dinner later, when suddenly, with no warning, the teacher turns out the lights and shows a horror movie.

Oh, it starts out innocently enough: There's a nice couple consisting of a woman who is pregnant and a man who is supportive-looking and who generally has a beard. They seem happy, but you just know she's going to go into labor. You want to stop her. It's exactly like those scary movies where the heroine goes down into the basement, and you want to shout, "DON'T GO DOWN INTO THE BASEMENT!" except in the childbirth class you want to shout, "DON'T GO INTO LABOR!"

But she always does go into labor. It seems to last a LOT longer than necessary. Hours turn into days, and still she is in labor. Outside her window, the seasons change. Her doctor grows old and gray and is eventually replaced by a new doctor, and STILL this poor woman is in labor. Her husband keeps telling her she's doing great, but you can tell from her expression that he's very lucky she doesn't have a ball-peen hammer.

Eventually, she becomes so deranged that she apparently does not even notice that there is a cameraperson shooting extreme footage of . . . OK, let's just say that it is not her most flattering angle.

When the woman gets to approximately her 15th year of labor, she begins making noises that you rarely hear outside of nature documentaries, and her husband edges back a little bit in case she gets her hands on a scalpel. The movie now becomes very explicit, causing the entire childbirth class to go into a mass cringe, all of us hunched up and involuntarily protecting as many of our body parts as possible. I use this time to practice my squinting, which is the most important thing the husband learns in childbirth class. I use a special Lamaze squinting technique that enables me to prevent virtually all rays of light from penetrating my eyeballs.

When the woman in the movie makes a noise identical to what you'd hear if a live yak went through a garlic press, I unsquint just enough to see it happen—the Blessed Event, the timeless miracle that makes the whole thing worthwhile:

An alien bursting out of the woman's chest cavity.

No, seriously, what happens is that the woman has a baby, via a process that makes what happened in *Alien* look like an episode of *Teletubbies*. Then our childbirth-class teacher turns the lights on, and the pregnant women all turn to face their husbands, and they all have the same facial expression, which says: "This is NOT fair."

We husbands respond by smiling supportively and patting their arms in a reassuring manner. Because we're sure they're going to do great.

Voyage of the Stuffed

I am a hearty, seafaring type of individual, so recently I spent a week faring around the sea aboard the largest cruise ship in the world that has not yet hit an iceberg. It is called the *Voyager*, and it weighs 140,000 tons, which is approximately the amount I ate in desserts alone.

The *Voyager* sails out of Miami every week carrying 3,200 passengers determined to relax or die trying. The ship has (I am not making any of this up) an ice-skating rink, a large theater, a shopping mall, a rock-climbing wall, and a nine-hole miniature golf course. We have come a long way indeed from the days when the Pilgrims crossed the Atlantic aboard the *Mayflower,* which—hard as it is to imagine today—had no skating rink and only four golf holes.

While aboard the ship, we passengers engaged in a wide range of traditional cruise-ship activities, including eating breakfast, snacking, eating lunch, drinking complex rum-based beverages while lying on deck absorbing solar radiation until we glowed like exit signs, snacking some more, eating dinner, eating more snacks, and passing out face-down in the pâté section of the midnight buffet.

Needless to say I did not attempt to climb the rock wall, which is good because the resulting disaster would have made for a chilling newspaper headline:

CRUISE SHIP EVACUATED AS MAN FALLS, EXPLODES;
Hundreds Spattered by Semi-digested Shrimp

The only stressful part of our shipboard routine was looking at photographs of ourselves. When you're on a cruise, photographers constantly pop up and take pictures of you; they put these on display in hopes that you'll buy them as souvenirs. At night, my wife and I would join the throng of passengers looking through the photos, hoping to find a nice flattering shot of ourselves, and then suddenly—YIKES—we'd be confronted with this terrifying image of two bloated, bright-red, slug-like bodies with OUR FACES. Jabba and Mrs. Hutt go to sea!

When every passenger had attained roughly the same body weight as a Buick Riviera, the ship would stop at a Caribbean island, and the passengers would waddle ashore to experience the traditional local culture, by which I mean shop for European jewelry and watches. I frankly don't know why it makes economic sense for a tourist from Montana to fly to Miami, get on a ship, and sail to Jamaica for the purpose of purchasing a watch made in Switzerland, but apparently it does, because shopping is very important to cruise passengers.

If these people ever get to Mars, they WILL expect to find jewelry stores.

The other thing you do when your ship is in port is take guided tours to Local Points of Interest. Under international law, every tour group must include one tourist who has the IQ of sod. In Jamaica, we toured a plantation, and our group included a woman whose brain operated on some kind of tape delay, as we see from this typical exchange between her and our guide:

GUIDE: These are banana plants, which produce bananas. You can see the bananas growing on these banana plants.

WOMAN (in a loud voice): What kind of plants are these?

GUIDE: Banana.

WOMAN: Huh! *(To her husband):* Frank, these are banana plants!

The woman repeated to Frank virtually everything the guide said. One day he will kill her with a kitchen appliance.

But I am proud to say that the winner of the award for Biggest Tourist Doofus was: me. What happened was, during the tour, a man demonstrated how he could climb a coconut tree using only a small rope made from twisted banana fibers. When he came down, he showed me the rope, and I, out of politeness, pretended to be interested in it, although in fact it was, basically, a rope. The man handed it to me and suggested I might want to "take it home to the kids." I frankly doubted that any modern Nintendo-raised American child would be thrilled by such a gift. ("Look, Timmy! A rope!") But I pretended to be grateful.

Then the man told me that such ropes USUALLY sell for $15 (he did not say where), but he would let it go for $10. And so, unable to figure out how to escape, I gave him $10. I imagine the other plantation workers laughed far into the night when he told them. ("He gave you $10 for the ROPE?" "Yes! He must be even stupider than the tape-delay woman!")

But don't get me wrong: I truly enjoyed the cruise. It was fun and relaxing, and it gave me a rare chance, amid all the hustle and bustle of my busy life, to pick up a substantial amount of body mass. Cruising is also romantic, so let me just say this to you couples out there: If you're looking for a way to rekindle the flame in your relationship, I'll sell you my rope.

My Workday: Nap, Toenail Inspection, Nap, Underwear Check, Nap

As a professional newspaper columnist with both medical AND dental benefits, I receive many letters from people who would like to get into my line of work.

"Dear Dave," they write. "I'm sick of my boring dead-end job as a (lawyer, teacher, office worker, Tipper Gore). How do I develop the skills I need to obtain a job like yours, where you have an opportunity to make a difference, even though you never actually do?"

OK, then: Today I'm going to take you "behind the scenes" here at Dave Barry Inc., and reveal, step-by-step, exactly how I write a column:

Step One is to come up with a topic. I am always thinking about possible topics, from the moment my alarm goes off at 6 A.M., through the moment I actually get out of the bed, at around 10:15. During that period I take a series of decompression naps while monitoring the morning TV news shows to find out what the news is. Unfortunately, the morning news shows no longer show the news: They're too busy showing the crowd of people who stand around outside the TV studio for hours on end waving at the camera and holding signs that say: "HI!" Evidently these people are too stupid to operate telephones, and this is the only way they have to communicate with their families or ward attendants back home. Sometimes the TV personalities go outside; I always hope that they'll point firearms at the sign-holders and yell, "GO HOME," but instead they ask the sign-holders where they're from. The fascinating answers never fail to amaze and delight everybody ("*Ohio??* Great!!").

So I have no column topic when I emerge from the bedroom to fix myself a hearty breakfast of coffee with extra coffee. My next step is to look through the daily newspaper, which I have found to be an invaluable and amazingly rich source of advertisements for women's underwear. Every other page has an ad featuring female models in lingerie; you get the impression, from newspapers, that at least 80 percent of the Gross National Product is brassieres. Why? Do women really need to be sold on the concept of underwear? Do they smack their foreheads and go, "THAT'S what I need! Something under my clothing!"?

But you can't write a professional column about women's underwear. You need a topic with some "meat" to it, such as the U.S. Trade Deficit, which is an important issue that the newspaper often puts next to the brassiere ads. And so, with this topic in mind, I head for my home office, which is an area that I would estimate, for tax purposes, covers 94 percent of the total square footage of my home.

I work at home because, as a professional writer, I find that a solitary environment enables me, whenever the muse strikes, to clip my toenails. This particular muse strikes more often than a French labor union. I'll be pondering the Trade Deficit, and I'll glance at my toenails and think, "Hey! Those babies have grown at LEAST three-thousandths of an inch since I last clipped them!" So I grab the clippers, which I always keep handy, and soon I'm hard at work. All your top writers do this. If you don't believe me, go up to, say, Norman Mailer, and have some friends hold him down while you remove his shoes and socks. If his toenails aren't trimmed to the base, I'll pay you $10. I'll need photographs.

Another reason why creative individuals prefer to work at home, as opposed to an office, is that when you need to scratch yourself, you don't have to sneak behind the copying machine and settle for a hasty grope. At home, you can rear back and assault the affected region with both hands, or, if you want, gardening implements.

But you cannot scratch yourself forever. You are not a professional baseball player; you are a newspaper columnist, and sooner or later you have to "knuckle down" and get to work on the task at hand, which is: lunch.

After lunch it's time to get back to thinking about the Trade Deficit. The key, with a complex issue like this, is:

research. A professional newspaper column has to be 800 words long, which is why I cannot say it enough: research, research, research. Among the questions that need to be answered are: What, exactly, IS the "Trade Deficit"? For this kind of technical detail, I get on the telephone to my Research Assistant, Judi Smith, a wealth of information.

"Judi," I say, "how come there are so many newspaper ads for women's underwear?"

"I think because men like to look at women in brassieres," she replies.

My wife, who also works at home and is listening to this discussion, notes: "All those ads look the same."

Both my wife and Judi agree that nobody ever buys a bra from an ad. It frankly makes me wonder if this could be a contributing factor to the Trade Deficit. Somebody should think about this. I'd do it, but these toenails are not getting any shorter.

Celebrate the aging process with this
New York Times **bestseller**

DAVE BARRY TURNS 50

(and he's not going to even *mention* "prostate")

Pop open a can of Geritol®, kick back in that recliner, grab those reading glasses, and let the good times roll—before they roll right over you! Dave Barry turns fifty and pinpoints the glaring signs that you've passed the half-century mark (You are suddenly unable to read anything written in letters smaller than Marlon Brando.).

This season, take your travel tips from Dave Barry, a guy who is really gone!

DAVE BARRY'S ONLY TRAVEL GUIDE YOU'LL EVER NEED. . .

. . . is complete with maps, histories, quaint local facts (France's National Underwear Changing Day is March 12), song lyrics, helpful hints on how to get through Customs (all insects must be spayed), and tidbits from Dave Barry's own fond vacation nightmares, including:

- Air Travel
(Or: Why Birds Never Look Truly Relaxed)

- Traveling as a Family
(Or: No, We Are NOT There Yet)

- Traveling in Europe
("Excuse me! Where is the Big Mona Lisa?")

- Camping: Nature's Way of Promoting the Motel Industry

"READ IT AND DIE LAUGHING."
—*New York Daily News*

Published by Ballantine Books.
Available wherever books are sold.

And don't miss the hilarious
New York Times bestseller:

DAVE BARRY'S COMPLETE GUIDE TO GUYS

For thousands of years, women have asked themselves: What is the deal with guys, anyway? What are they thinking? The answer, of course, is: virtually nothing. But that has not stopped Dave Barry from writing an entire book about them, dealing frankly and semi-thoroughly with such important guy issues as:

- Scratching

- Why the average guy can remember who won the 1960 World Series but not necessarily the names of all his children

- Why guys cannot simultaneously think and look at breasts

- Why guys prefer to believe that there is no such thing as a "prostate"

"[A] LAUGH-OUT-LOUD BOOK."
—People

Published by Ballantine Books.
Available wherever books are sold.